Assessment in the Service of Learning

Proceedings of the
1987 ETS Invitational Conference

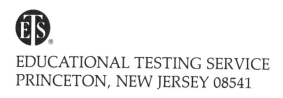

EDUCATIONAL TESTING SERVICE
PRINCETON, NEW JERSEY 08541

The forty-eighth ETS Invitational Conference, sponsored
by Educational Testing Service, was held at The Plaza,
New York City, on October 31, 1987.

Presiding: Gregory R. Anrig
            President
            Educational Testing Service

Conference Coordinator: Margaret B. Lamb

Proceedings Editor: Eileen E. Freeman

Production: Eric Coolidge

Library of Congress Catalog Number: ISBN 0-88685-070-3

Contents

The 1987 ETS Award for Distinguished Service to Measurement

Presented to
KARL G. JÖRESKOG

Factor analysis has long served as an exploratory technique to search for explanatory constructs underlying observed relationships. Karl G. Jöreskog demonstrated how factor analysis can also serve as a confirmatory technique to test statistically whether measures of particular hypothesized constructs indeed yield data consistent with the theoretical expectations. In integrating exploratory and confirmatory aspects of factor analysis in a general model, Professor Jöreskog provided the mathematical foundations for rigorous statistical estimation, as well as for coping systematically with perennial problems of factor identification. Indeed, his general model so unifies the field that the only reason for teaching factor analysis and related techniques in any other terms would be for historical purposes.

Even more profound and far-reaching is the integration of factor analysis with "causal" or path analysis afforded by Professor Jöreskog's Linear Structural Relations approach, which is popularly known as LISREL. The LISREL framework is more than just a general analytical technique. It provides a powerful mode of thinking about theory construction, measurement problems, and data analysis that promises to make the social sciences both more precise and more cumulative. When a LISREL model adequately accounts for the obtained findings, it facilitates causal inferences from observational or nonexperimental data. Such causal inferences are of a type that social scientists have long aspired to but have rarely had rigorous evidence to sustain. The LISREL framework also applies to the simultaneous analysis of data from numerous groups and to the analysis of data from the same group obtained on different occasions. It thereby yields a unified approach to the issues of factorial invariance, structural change, and differential causal theories.

For his seminal integrative models systematizing the structure of measurement and causal relationships, of group differences, and of longitudinal change, and for his landmark contributions to statistical estimation and hypothesis testing in these areas, ETS is pleased to present its 1987 Award for Distinguished Service to Measurement to Karl G. Jöreskog.

ETS Award for Distinguished Service to Measurement, Recipients, 1970-1987

1970 E. F. Lindquist

1971 Lee J. Cronbach

1972 Robert L. Thorndike

1973 Oscar K. Buros

1974 J. P. Guilford

1975 Harold Gullikson

1976 Ralph W. Tyler

1977 Anne Anastasi

1978 John C. Flanagan

1979 Robert C. Ebel

1980 John B. Carroll

1981 Ledyard R Tucker

1982 Raymond B. Cattell

1983 Frederic M. Lord

1984 Louis Guttman
     Henry Chauncey (special award)

1985 Paul Horst

1986 Frederic Kuder

1987 Karl G. Jöreskog

How Assessment Can Best Serve Teaching and Learning

BILL HONIG
Superintendent of Public Instruction, State of California

Today I would like to discuss some of the issues in testing that we are addressing in California. Before we can talk about assessment, we must have a good grasp of exactly what we want children to learn. One of the objections to the assessment program is that it drives the curriculum. However, that is not bad, if we think through exactly where we want that curriculum to go. Every one of our educational reform efforts in California is grounded on a strong understanding of what we want to happen to children. Three major purposes guide the direction we are taking.

Our first goal is widely agreed upon throughout the country—we must educate our students to higher levels of literacy than ever before so that they can compete in the job market and so that our nation can remain competitive in the world economy. We are not just talking about the college-bound students. We are talking about high standards and expectations for all our students.

Clearly, the job market is changing rapidly. WORK FORCE 2000, recently published by the Hudson Institute for the U. S. Department of Labor, describes the kinds of jobs that we will be facing in 13 years when children now entering kindergarten will be graduating. The researchers did something interesting, which I do not think has been done before—they took every job in the United States, categorized them, and then ranked them according to educational demand. What standards will be required to handle each type of job? The researchers found 57 categories of education. Right now about 24 percent of the jobs are in the top three categories. By the year 2000, that number will jump to over 40 percent. This shift in educational requirements for the work force means we are going to have to apply the techniques that we used for the college-bound to more of our students than ever before.

The second objective of our educational reform effort is to prepare young people for their roles as citizens. We just published a history framework in California with very specific guidelines about how to prepare our young people to accept their role as citizens. We are saying students should take three years of world history and three years of American history. There should be more in-depth study of people and basic documents and a very clear understanding of how this democracy works. We cannot teach the principles of democracy in just one twelfth-grade civics course. Teaching about democracy is not merely an intellectual exercise; the emotional allegiance must also be developed.

The third point is a little more controversial, although it is interesting that two of the best sellers—*Cultural Literacy* by E. D. Hirsch and *The Closing of the American Mind* by Allan Bloom—are addressing this issue. Every child, whether or not he or she goes to college, has a right to be cultured and to develop the breadth of understanding necessary to have free choice.

There is now strong agreement that this objective is a legitimate part of what we need in the schools. We have a tremendous amount of freedom in this country. Individuals have the liberty to make choices, but that freedom is a sham unless we also develop people's understanding and their ability to choose. People cannot choose from ignorance; they have to choose from an educated perspective. That is the whole idea behind a liberal education. Character development, the understanding of how the world works—both politically and socially—all that cultural understanding is essential for a young person to be integrated into society.

These three goals, then, have guided our curriculum reform efforts in California. Once one adopts these three objectives—job preparation and civic and cultural understanding—one can get on with the task of fashioning the curriculum and support systems to achieve those ends.

Professor Allan Odden of the University of Southern California has looked at some of the effects of California's reform movement in those schools where it has been successful. He found some interesting points, which he will be publishing in a study soon. He found that what is happening in successful schools is that several major initiatives have come together to make them successful—the curriculum guidelines, the general objectives, the testing program, staff development, and the training of principals. Each activity has reinforced the others, and the curriculum has become aligned.

Now I would like to talk about how assessment can support the mission that we have undertaken in a variety of ways. The first thing we did in California was to revamp the tests in the state, because they were based on too narrow a notion of the curriculum. Essentially, they were basic skill tests. They were similar to those used in most parts of the country where statewide testing using multiple-choice problems is the norm, although California's tests were broader. We had a third-, sixth-, and twelfth-grade test that we gave each year in California to test basic skills. Our current testing program uses matrix tests. There are 32 different booklets, and students answer 10 or 12 questions in a half-hour period once a year. They do not all answer all the questions. The questions are spread across the board, so it is not a test of the individual; it is, however, a valid test of how well that school and the state are doing in each area.

We had a big gap between the sixth-grade and the twelfth-grade testing programs, so one of the first things that I did when I became superintendent was to see that an eighth-grade test was developed that included two additional components in science and history. In addition, we now ask students for a writing sample in the eighth and twelfth grades. We are giving strong feedback to the schools to let them know what we are going to assess, and that information has had a major impact on what is taught.

Currently, we have good data on what students are actually taking in the state. Before we started our reform effort in 1983, about 40 percent of eighth graders took science; now enrollment is up around 54 percent. That is a fairly hefty jump. The increase is partly because of the tests and partly because we are holding the schools accountable for their enrollments. That increase is the good news. The bad news is that one-half of all eighth graders are not taking science, so we still have a long way to go. We are in the process of adding science to the sixth-grade tests, which will further enhance the elementary school curriculum.

The second issue we addressed was what is called higher-order thinking skills—designing problems that demand a higher level of response. There have been two arguments in testing. One argument, made by Jim Popham about 10 years ago, was that a test question needs a narrow focus so that only one response is appropriate. The problem with that approach is that it sends a fragmented and narrow message to the people who are developing the tests. We are looking for a combination of abilities to answer the questions. We have included some open-ended questions that require students to think—whether it is in history or in math. That is some of the technical work started at the eighth grade. We have revised the twelfth-grade test along similar lines.

Our eighth- and twelfth-grade tests are now powerful. Commercial tests have not added new or harder questions, and—as some commentators have said—it is interesting that the whole country is above the 50th percentile. Every single report is always above grade level. Part of that critique is that the students get to know the questions after a while. The advantage of the large pool of questions administered on the matrix sampling basis in California is that teachers are forced to coach the students on more than a thousand questions at a grade level—not an impossible task, but one that, when attempted, may actually look more like curriculum reform than test coaching. The outcome, therefore, is considerably more gradual growth and, we assume, more realistic assessment of our program.

The argument we are dealing with is testing time and individual test scores. There is always a tension between giving individual data back to the school for children and the data that we need at the state level. With modern testing techniques, it is possible to do both. We can have a local test tailored for local needs and can imbed the questions that we need for the state. We have called this approach a Comprehensive Assessment System (CAS). We met with some of the publishing companies initially; money was to be allocated by the legislature twice for this CAS, but it was vetoed by the governor. We became frustrated and decided to try to do it on our own. Tom Boysen, who is now the county superintendent in San Diego, took the lead in organizing about 20 districts to put money in the pot, so they had quite a sizable fund. They designed a testing program that is now being piloted. The beauty of CAS is that it provides continuity, individual scores, and a lot more flexibility. We are talking to several test-publishing companies about trying this out.

The third area I would like to talk about is very exciting for the educational community and deals with developing a proficiency scale for our tests. We have examples every day in the newspaper of the importance of this information. For instance, AT&T gave a test to 2,000 applicants and only 16 passed. Industry is asking, "Are you getting students above a certain level? And are they qualified to do the job?" We should be able to say exactly what is it that we are hoping for when we hire somebody. Then we have something we can strive for—how many students can we get to that particular level?

NAEP has done that. Let's take the last NAEP reading assessment. There is a scale of reading proficiency based on test items. An adept level is close to the real world. What can you do with performance-based tests as opposed to grade-level reporting? Some of the items are very similar, but a performance-based test can tell you whether a person can read an article in *The New York Times* and understand it.

We need to have industry come up with "power items." They are the opposite of argument testing. We want to make sure these tests give

4

curriculum messages—this is what to teach and this is what our students should be able to do. But these skills should not stop at literacy; they should include mathematics, science, writing, history, and philosophy. Twelfth graders should be able to explain what democracy is all about, and we can develop a scale to see how effectively they understand it. We need to work on this issue. The test should be almost like a foreign service exam—how much do students know about how things work?

The next step is to take those six or seven items and figure out scales of performance. If we start doing that nationally, it will be a powerful force pushing curriculum in the right direction because it will be a performance test. We should, as a nation, set a goal if we are going to compete economically in this modern technological world. We cannot get by with 40 percent of our students at the adept reading level. We have to go to 60 percent. We need to set a national goal. Then we have the state and school reading levels, and we can go right back to the schools and tell them they should have the following percentages of their kids above this level, and that everybody should go up 50 percent in the next five or 10 years. Once we have an understanding of what we have to do, we can concentrate on how to get to it. We have the assessment in place that confirms, reinforces, and supports the curriculum. The purpose of the national goals is not just to compare one state to another but to compare how we are doing on a common mission.

The other thing you can do for California relates to our accountability program. The program not only looks at testing but at other aspects of a school and how a school compares to schools with similar student populations. We have a whole series of measures that we call quality indicators. The accountability program is a very effective tool. When we find two schools with the same kind of student body getting very different results, we know something is wrong at the lower-performing school. That school is not doing the job, and we have to figure out what the problem is. Nobody can say that their school cannot succeed because of the students—they have examples of successful schools with similar students staring them in the face. Any accountability program can be a healthy management tool, but to do it you have to get these skills in place and get agreement about the general targets. They cannot be too hard or too soft; they must be realistic.

The fourth issue is that the type of test items also drives the curriculum. In England they have designed very sophisticated test items for science, mathematics, and languages, and they are at the point where they can have an assessment of how well students address a problem. You can watch it—it is a technically sophisticated way of judging. Every student answers every question. How do they deal with a science problem? Those kinds of test questions are going to drive the curriculum in a different direction than multiple-choice questions. Therefore, we should sprinkle more sophisticated questions in our tests or shift in some degree so the tests do not just compare students at the lower level. Students must have enough depth of understanding to be able to do well on these kinds of questions, and that evolves with time. Some people want every question to be this kind of open-ended question. They recoil when one puts in a straight addition or division problem in a test. I disagree with that as well.

The fifth issue we are dealing with is the Golden State Exam. This test is similar to the Regents' Exams in New York. Under Senate Bill 813, California's Educational Reform Act of 1983, the State Department of Education has been given responsibility for developing achievement tests. The tests are for the average child—not necessarily the college-bound. They are supposed to allow the average child to excel. We are just starting to develop the exams in these areas. We now have algebra, geometry, and U.S. history. We are supposed to develop 16 tests when funding becomes available. Schools and students voluntarily take the exams, and they seem to be very popular in California. There are no scholarships attached to them yet, but the tests seem to be effective instruments to push for quality in the subject areas. They reach large numbers of young people. As students start to take these tests, the achievement level and motivation at the high school will begin to go up.

The sixth issue I would like to raise is that of other tests that obviously are of vital interest—specifically the Carnegie Corporation's concept of teacher certification. We are working on how to prepare and assess teachers coming into the system. This topic is under discussion in our state and around the country; a lot of work is going on regarding how we can best prepare and assess teachers. We are going to need 160,000 new teachers in California in the next nine years. Do they have the breadth of knowledge necessary to teach the enhanced curriculum? Are they well-enough prepared? Our curriculum calls for three years of world history. Do our teachers have the necessary background to teach that and other subjects? We will need assessment tests for teachers, plus other forms of review.

The final issue is ensuring that reforms are implemented at the school site. The reform movement is at the point now where we have begun to upgrade textbooks; we are pushing for curriculum quality; we are developing training. All these different portions are battling for resources, but it really is up to each school to put this reform movement together with the district's support. We need teachers who can teach this curriculum; we need to address the dropout problem; we need to work on restructuring at the school site. To be successful we must take two very important steps.

First, we must reach a consensus about what we mean by quality. If we are going to accredit schools, we must know what makes a quality school. For too long in this country people have refused to talk about quality. They want to talk about process issues instead. We are very close to defining quality in California, where we have a program review document and a good consensus about what we want in our schools. Second, once we know what we are looking for, how do we judge whether it is there or not? There must be a working agreement on both method of judgment and assessment and how to go about it. That is a lot easier said than done. Part of it is judgmental, and there is nothing wrong with exercising professional judgment. Most of you can walk into a school and in three minutes know whether or not it is a great school. You know things are going right.

If we can get a definition of quality—and agreement on how we are going to assess it—then we have an outcome-based performance system. That means there has to be some professional work in the country and at the university on exactly how we define those criteria. That will be a very interesting and exciting task. Rochester, New York, schools are breaking new ground along these lines. They have a career ladder for teachers that ranges from interns to "lead" teachers. The teachers will have more power in return for being held more accountable. If you look back at what we did in the 1970s, it is clear that states tested teachers or master teachers much too narrowly. The tests really did not measure all the skills and knowledge a teacher must have. On the other hand, complete decentralization that permits a teacher to do whatever he or she wants does not work, either.

Peters and Waterman had a very good component that states the issue perfectly—they call it a simultaneously loose and tightened management system. You define what you want in general so that people have the same definition and a carbon copy of the same general accomplishments, but you are loose enough so that you have flexibility in implementation. It is a great trick if you can pull it off, but it calls for very good leadership on the part of principals and districts.

It does not make sense that we are in education and we do not have a consensus about what we mean by quality in an elementary school. There is a tremendous feeling in education that we cannot define quality school-by-school, because each situation is so different. A teacher in

Eureka feels that the circumstances are very different from those in Los Angeles—that a rural area is totally unlike an urban area. My response to that argument is this is a national society and certain things—like democracy, Thomas Jefferson, and biology—are important no matter where you are. We have a responsibility to convey this knowledge to our students. We have three needs—economic, democratic, and cultural—and we cannot have a society in which some students get this information and others do not.

These next few years are going to be some of the most creative in assessment. For the first time we will have a chance to determine what we want to teach, how we assess it, and where we want to go, and then develop the training, staff development, and support to reach these goals. If we have all these engines pushing in the same direction, we can change how much students learn, and I hope to see that happen.

Progress in Measurement, Cognitive Science, and Technology That Can Change the Relation Between Instruction and Assessment

RICHARD E. SNOW
Stanford University

The title assigned to me for this conference implies that there has been progress in the three identified domains that can change the relation between instruction and assessment—presumably to unite them in the service of learning—if we are willing to work toward this end. I believe that there has indeed been such progress, and some strong R&D programs have now indeed turned to the task of uniting instruction and assessment—C. Victor Bunderson's new program at ETS is a clear case in point. So there is a good base for optimism.

In educational measurement in recent decades, the development of item-response models, new equating and bias-detection procedures, confirmatory factor analysis, and a host of other improvements have made educational and psychometric measurements stronger and more useful today than ever before. Over the same period, a new view of substantive psychology in education has grown up. Cognitive psychology and computer science have attacked the problem of *mind*, not only in the laboratory, but increasingly in the medium of real-world cognitive performance, including school-learning performance. The new cognitive theories attempt to explain complex knowledge and skill acquisition, organization, and use, and also individual differences therein, at a level of content and process detail that is beginning to provide a stronger and more useful instructional psychology.

Increasingly coupled with these two developments has been the rapid growth of computer technology, including associated audio, video, and even tactile technology, to permit automated adaptive instructional presentation and sequencing, adaptive testing, adaptive item construction and banking, intelligent tutors, and simulations of amazingly complex

9

systems for instructional purposes. It does appear that the technology exists now, or is at least feasible in the near future, to bring instruction and assessment together.

In order to do it right, however, we must learn how to use psychometric and substantive advances in consort. This is the main challenge, in my view. A flood of reviews and discussions of this issue have appeared recently. For example, the 1985 ETS Invitational Conference concerned "The Redesign of Testing for the 21st Century" (Freeman, 1986). The last two Buros Institute symposia also addressed the future of testing and the cognitive psychology of testing (Plake & Witt, 1986; Ronning, Glover, Conoley, & Witt, in press). David Lohman of the University of Iowa and I have also written a large chapter for Linn's third edition of *Educational Measurement*, in which we attempt to identify the implications of cognitive psychology for educational measurement (Snow & Lohman, in press). There are many other references. I could not reiterate, or even summarize, all of the interesting ideas, promises, projections, cautions, and criticisms that have already been published, even if I had unlimited space. I urge you to read some of this literature as an appendix to this brief paper.

What I can do here instead is propose a crude taxonomy for tracking present progress and then examine several examples to suggest what has been done and what remains to be done. Finally, I discuss three of the more general problems that need to be addressed as work continues.

My crude scheme has two facets. The first identifies five educational functions that must be served in any instructional and assessment system. For short, I use the old conventional labels:

1. Aptitude profile assessment

2. Direct aptitude development

3. Counseling and guidance

4. Instructional treatment design and evaluation

5. Achievement profile assessment

It should be clear, however, that these labels refer to functions, not to existing definitions, instruments, or procedures. Thus, for example, "aptitude assessment" does not refer simply to conventional tests; it refers to measures of learning skills, strategies, styles, attitudes, prior knowledge (including misconceptions relevant to upcoming instruction), and perceptions of the situation and the self as a learner. "Achievement assessment" includes measures of cognitive and motivational structure—how one thinks about and uses instructional content both in and beyond instruction—not just conventional tests of facts and concepts. "Profile" signifies that both aptitude and achievement are always multivariate. "Counseling and guidance" refers not only to guidance in course choice, but also to instructional treatment or materials choice—to guided learner control over instruction and over self as a learner, not just to academic and vocational counseling through interest inventories.

The second facet represents the view that any instructional and assessment system must be adaptive to individual learners' needs and characteristics (Cronbach & Snow, 1977; Glaser, 1977). To keep it simple, I use two levels: "macroadaptation," referring to adjustments to fit learner needs from month to month or from year to year, and "microadaption," referring to adjustments from minute to minute or day to day. Obviously, there is a macro-micro continuum, not just two levels.

Although one can think of this scheme as a 2x5 classification to consider examples in each cell, I prefer to think of it as a kind of wagon wheel, as shown in Figure 1. The rim represents macroadaptation and the

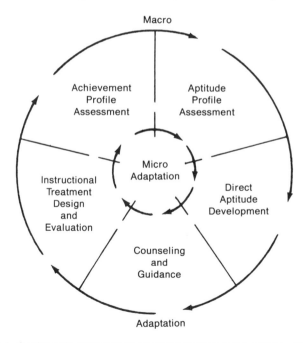

Macro

Achievement Profile Assessment

Aptitude Profile Assessment

Micro Adaptation

Instructional Treatment Design and Evaluation

Direct Aptitude Development

Counseling and Guidance

Adaptation

Figure 1. A schematic taxonomy of adaptive functions in the relation of instruction and assessment

11

hub, microadaptation; the spokes partition the five functions. I prefer this representation because the five functions have traditionally operated more or less in a cyclical time order: Aptitude assessment precedes attempts at aptitude development; counseling follows aptitude assessment and precedes instructional treatment; achievement assessment follows instructional treatment but becomes aptitude assessment for further instruction.

For some time, we have had a semblance of macroadaptive education, at least in parts of the wheel. Aptitude assessments predict achievement and provide a crude form of readiness diagnosis, to indicate when, for example, a special program should be used to develop needed aptitude for regular instructional treatment. Traditional counseling helps the learner shape subsequent courses of study. What the progress in measurement, cognitive science, and technology now allows us to do is to spiral in toward more microadaptive systems, wherein the partitions between the traditional five functions begin to blur. This does not eliminate macroadaptation, because that is needed, too, and there has also been progress toward connecting instruction and assessment at this level. But microadaptation has not before been possible, except in the flow of expert human teaching.

I like to think of two wheels in Figure 1, one for automated instructional and assessment systems, and one for human teachers as instructional and assessment systems. The two will have to move in synchrony, each using information coming from the other. The best adaptive education systems of the future will have that communication link between teacher and computer as an integral feature. Calfee and Wang have much to say about the teacher side of such systems elsewhere in this volume.

Now I can step through the five functions around the wheel to consider examples of research that begin to show how microadaptive instructional and assessment systems might be designed. Where possible, I choose examples in each function category that connect with those in others. These connections, however, are still patchy, given the present state of the work.

Aptitude profile assessment

For the past decade or so, research in a number of laboratories has sought to analyze the information-processing activities involved in performance on cognitive tasks. The tasks studied have included both the laboratory tasks of cognitive science and many of the ability tests typically used as indicants of cognitive aptitude for learning.

A new style theory of aptitude has emerged, with three principal findings: First, it is possible to identify and isolate at least some of the component processing skills required in ability-test performance. Stimulus encoding, feature comparison, rule induction, rule application, and response justification are examples of such separable processes (see, e.g., Lohman, in press; Pellegrino & Glaser, 1982; Sternberg, 1985). Second, it has been shown that a significant portion of individual difference variance reflected in such tests arises from strategic adaptation of information processing during performance, not just from constituent skill differences, i.e., individuals shift strategies as a function of item characteristics and adapt these strategies as they learn through the task (see, e.g., Bethell-Fox, Lohman, & Snow, 1984; Kyllonen, Lohman, & Woltz, 1984; Snow & Lohman, 1984). Third, new sources of variation in ability and learning task performance have been identified that are not primarily skill or strategy differences; the attentional requirements of tasks, and the degree to which constituent processing becomes automatic with practice, are examples (see, e.g., Ackerman, 1987; Hunt & Lansman, 1982).

What emerges is a description of reasoning- or verbal- or spatial-ability tests — and increasingly also of learning and problem-solving tasks — as dynamic microprocessing models. In effect, the research provides a new and elaborated form of construct validation for aptitude assessments (see Snow & Lohman, in press, for a review).

This progress in the cognitive psychology of testing is now coupled with progress in measurement. Embretson's (1985) multicomponent latent-trait models, for example, bring the separate component process identifications into combination in the most powerful psychometric model. Also, Mislevy and Verhelst (1986) have adapted IRT models to handle some of the problems posed by strategy variation in test performance. Butterfield and his colleagues (1985) have shown how the cognitive analyses lead to computerized item-generation procedures designed to control the various sources of item difficulty — in effect, to control the cognitive psychology of the test — more precisely and more adaptively than human item writers do. In short, the aptitude profiles become microdiagnostic and the assessment instruments become microadaptive to the needs of the rest of the system.

Direct aptitude development

With the microdiagnosis of aptitude in hand, it should be possible to build training treatments that help develop the constituents of aptitude directly. Several research projects have been pursuing this, but Frederiksen's (1981, 1982, 1985ab) work on reading is a particularly good example of this line of progress because it also shows how to combine the cognitive psychology of verbal processing with powerful psychometric methods, such as LISREL-based factor analysis. Also, reading is an especially important case, because it is both an educational goal in itself and an aptitude for learning in other domains.

Frederiksen distinguishes three types of information-processing skills important for reading:

1. **word analysis processes** (e.g., encoding single and multiletter units, translating graphemic units into phonological units, and activating appropriate lexical categories);

2. **discourse analysis processes** (e.g., retrieving and integrating word meanings, comprehending basic propositions underlying sentences, integrating processes across sentences, resolving problems of reference, and inferring nonexplicit but essential relations by elaborating to prior knowledge); and

3. **integrative processes** (e.g., generating extrapolations from the text models, combining information from perceptual and contextual sources).

These three types of component processes interact because they share processing resources and work on a common data base. Components also differ in the degree to which they have been automated; skilled readers show more and better component automation than less-skilled readers.

The construction and validation of such a battery proceeds in several steps. First, tasks hypothesized to require particular components are selected. Second, stimulus variables are identified that can be manipulated to alter the processing difficulty of the designated components. Third, contrasts among task conditions are computed for each person to represent the extent to which performance is degraded as stimulus variables are manipulated. Predicted declines in performance constitute a first-level validation of the task and its process model. Convergent and discriminant validity of individual contrast scores constitutes the second level of validation. This is accomplished through the formation and testing of a set of structural equations using LISREL.

Frederiksen (1982) developed measures for eight of these component processes, tested several models for component interactions, and then correlated the component measures with a range of reference ability tests. His analysis indicates that conventional tests of reading speed, vocabulary, and comprehension do not include some important discourse-processing skills.

With the initial battery assembled, Frederiksen then selected three of the eight components for training. Selection was based on two criteria: performance on the component should influence higher-level components, and automatic performance of the component should significantly reduce the drain on processing resources required by other components. Components thus selected were: perception of multiletter units within words, decoding orthographic patterns to phonological units of speech, and context utilization. Computer games were then devised to train each skill. Extensive study of poor readers showed that training was effective for some subjects on some components.

Frederiksen's work is ongoing and will be strengthened by larger validation and training studies. Nevertheless, it is a prime example of the sort of improvements to educational measurement that can be produced by combining sophisticated measurement models with good cognitive theory. It also shows the integration of aptitude assessment and aptitude training.

Achievement profile assessment

Now jump back to achievement profile assessment and consider that side of the wheel. Cognitive analysis has also been carried out to understand the declarative and procedural knowledge structures produced by instruction, the kinds of errors learners make during as well as after instruction, and the various forms of misconceptions they harbor that interfere with learning progress. Much of the work has been done on mathematics and science, but work in other school subjects is beginning.

What emerges from this work are models of knowledge structure and its acquisition that constitute new theories of achievement. There are implications that different kinds of instruction can produce qualitatively different kinds of cognitive structures. Research has begun to look

15

beyond the achievement goals of a given course, in mathematics, for example, to ask what it means to think mathematically—to transfer mathematical knowledge beyond the situation given (Greeno, 1986).

The knowledge-structure research suggests several kinds of associated assessment methods. The work of J. Brown and Burton (1978) shows how tasks can be designed for error diagnosis. Resnick's (1984) work suggests how strategic inventions reflecting understanding might be assessed. Greeno and Mayer (1975) demonstrate the use of faceted achievement tests to detect qualitative cognitive structural differences. There are many other ideas about achievement assessment in this line of research (see, e.g., Glaser, Lesgold, & Lajoie, in press).

One of the best examples of diagnostic achievement assessment is the research of A. Brown and Campione (1986) and their colleagues (see, e.g., Brown & Ferrara, 1985; Campione & Brown, 1984; Campione, Brown, Ferrara, Jones, & Sternberg, 1985; Ferrara, Brown, & Campione, 1986). Their procedure is to administer sets of problems, from theory-based achievement tests in arithmetic, for example, or even from ability tests such as Raven matrices or letter series, and then to provide hints to the learner when difficulties occur. The hint-giving is designed in a hierarchical structure from general to specific to assess the amount of instruction each individual needs to solve a problem. The tasks are arranged to provide measures of learning gain and also transfer distance (i.e., how different a transfer problem could be and still be solved).

Their results show that learning and transfer measures are related to conventional ability tests, but are better predictors of independently measured pre-post gains in achievement, and provide diagnostic information not available from the conventional tests. It appears, furthermore, that measures of flexible or "far" transfer offer particularly useful prediction and diagnosis. The work further implicates the importance of metacognitive thinking skills in learning and transfer.

A further example, from Novick (1986), also deserves special note, because it demonstrates both positive and negative transfer in analogical reasoning on test-like mathematical word problems; it also emphasizes assessment of the procedures used by students, not just solution time or accuracy. Novick's experiments manipulate the order of problem presentation so that a preceding problem and a target problem might have analogically related deep structures but unrelated surface structures, or vice versa. Students are also prompted with suggested solution procedures. These are between-person experiments, but within-person tests could be built on the same principles.

16

With measures of the kinds of solution procedures actually used on target problems, Novick demonstrates that more able students transfer efficient procedures from previous problems, whereas less able students do not. He also shows that students of intermediate ability perform like more able students when analogous problems are close in time to target problems, and like less able students when related problems are not close in time. Furthermore, students at all ability levels show negative transfer when surface properties of different problems are closely similar, but this sort of negative transfer is much less prevalent for the more able students. The differences are attributable to the cognitive representations of deep and surface features of problems by persons differing in ability and to their transfer of solution procedures based on these representations. The research leads not only to a performance model of analogical transfer (see also Holyoak, 1984), but also to a procedure for assessing such transfer.

Instructional treatment design and evaluation

Just as the cognitive analysis of aptitude leads to the design of direct aptitude training, so the cognitive analysis of achievement leads to the evaluation and redesign of instructional treatments. Intelligent tutors are already being designed to detect and remediate sources of arithmetic errors at a microadaptive level. Sequences of examples used in textbooks or by teachers are being studied to determine if their design and juxtaposition promote the kinds of inferences needed for optimal learning in algebra and geometry. Similarly, the structure of text is being examined to determine the degree to which it promotes the intended cognitive structures in learners and how the metacognitive strategies needed for comprehension monitoring can be better promoted. Learning-strategy training is now also added to the design to help learners construct useful cognitive organizations during text reading.

The example that comes closest today to a clear demonstration of how both aptitude and achievement assessments can be used interactively with instructional design and sequencing comes from the work of Lesgold and his colleagues (see Lesgold, Bonar, & Ivill, 1987; see also Lesgold & Gott in this volume). As a bridge, I use a mixture of Lesgold's terminology and mine.

An instructional system on electricity builds up a model of learner knowledge through close cycles of instruction and testing. The model is based on a curriculum goal structure and shows an achievement profile, i.e., the state of each goal acquisition for that learner, at any point in time. Rules govern which part of the profile to work on next. As instruction proceeds, a diagnostic cycle sweeps through the student profile, or model, to identify the parts that should next be tested and to produce test problems suited to that student according to a list of constraints on item type or format. These constraints are based partly on an aptitude profile and partly on the need to detect bugs or misconceptions so that they can be corrected before instruction proceeds.

An example item might be: "Test use of Ohm's Law in diagrammed circuits, but use simple computations because this student is still weak in numerical skill." In other words, because instruction cannot work on the whole achievement profile at once, it sidesteps some weaknesses while instructing and testing others. In short, the system of microadaptive rules for coordinated instruction and test design comes closer to integrating the four upper parts of the wheel in Figure 1 than any other system today, at least to my knowledge.

Counseling and guidance

Counseling and guidance is here left until last because it has so far received the least attention. It should not, however, be ignored. At the macro level, there are already advances such as SIGI PLUS, the self-contained interactive system for values clarification developed at ETS. But instructional automation allows several kinds of microadaption, usually by giving the learner control over instructional sequences and alternatives. Learner choices presumably express personal interests, preferences, and needs. "Learner control" has indeed been an advertised advantage of computerized instruction.

I classify this form of microadaptation as counseling and guidance because I believe that learner instructional choices should be informed or guided by assessments; learners may often not know what is best for them (Snow, 1980a). But what form these assessments should take is not yet clear. Presumably, different mixtures of task choice by the learner and task assignment based on aptitude and achievement assessments will be needed at different points as instruction proceeds. We know precious little about microadaptive counseling and guidance at the present time. Studying human teachers (and tutors) in this regard might well be instructive.

Some new lines of research also suggest the tailoring of instructional content based on learner interests and motivational characteristics.

18

Anderson and his colleagues (1987) are studying how interesting reading material is perceived at the level of sentences and paragraphs. They find marked effects on learning based on students' rated interest, and marked gender differences in this, incidentally. Lepper and Malone (1987; see also Malone & Lepper, 1987) study the design factors in computerized educational games that make them more or less intrinsically motivating. Individual differences related to learning are likely to be found here, too. It is easy to see the next step into tailored paragraphs and presentation features, based on assessments of student characteristics and expressed preferences. Despite all these progressive steps, three problems will impede or even defeat progress if they are not addressed. I call these the problems of tractability, proximal goals, and conation.

The problem of tractability. It is one thing to progress from macro- to micro-adaptive systems through cognitive analysis of aptitude, instruction, achievement, and counseling. But how "micro" must we get? As Pellegrino and Glaser (1979) pointed out some years ago, we have the problem of finding the level of analysis that is most instructionally tractable.

We have the same problem in finding the level of "graininess" that is most useful for assessment. This is not necessarily the most micro level possible, and it may not be the same level for different kinds of knowledge and skill, or for different assessment purposes. If we do not reach down to the right level, we fail to capture important components of learning process. If we reach too far down, we fail to capture important organizational and strategic features of learning process (see Snow, 1980b; Snow & Lohman, 1984).

In either case, both instruction and assessment will miss the mark of most progress. Tractability also implies ease of handling and thus economy of system design. Do intelligent tutors really need to be designed to detect and correct all possible types of errors, for example? Must an aptitude test assess all known component skills? No one has answers to these sorts of questions yet.

The problem of proximal goals. A related problem concerns the specification of instructional goals at a level too close to the instruction at hand. There are two aspects to this problem. First, if the goal structure is conditioned only by immediate course content, it is likely to leave out the long-range transfer objectives — the thinking like a mathematician — that may be the most important instructional outcomes to study (Greeno,

19

1986). Rather different instructional and assessment designs are often implied when retention and transfer criteria are studied, but research rarely includes such criteria. Second, if the goal structure is assumed to be domain-specific, then the new instructional-assessment designs may become encapsulated—one might say entombed—in the existing curriculum structure. But suppose that for some purposes, it is best to learn mathematics in the context of physics, or engineering, or business—or to learn history via art and geography. Rather different instructional and assessment designs would occur to us if there were no walls between curriculum domains.

The problem of conation. Last comes perhaps the biggest problem, already implied in what could—or rather, what could not—be said under "counseling and guidance" above.

Conation means "purposeful striving" —one might even say "will power." It is the part of the ancient trilogy of psychology—cognition, conation, affection—that has been largely left out of U.S. psychology for many decades (Snow & Farr, 1987). Motivation, volition, action, control, will—all are aspects of conation. Just because progress in cognitive measurement, cognitive science, and cognitive technology has been so fast, most of conation has been neglected, at least by most researchers. Those who design intelligent tutors sometimes seem not to realize that the learner is a human being. Most human learners will not do several hundred arithmetic problems so that the tutor can build up a model of them. Nor can most humans bear to be praised or corrected using the same phrases over and over again. Human learners are idiosyncratic, playful, second-guessers. They get bored, tired, fidgety, humorous, entranced, turned-on, ingenious, dedicated, and all the other adjectives that display humanness.

Mark Lepper (1987) at Stanford is trying to design an "empathetic" tutor. His question is: What can be built into the technology to make it as humanely interpersonal as possible? He relates an observation that is symptomatic of the present state of cognitive science. The Stanford Psychology Department has a huge computerized dictionary of psychological terms, so that research papers can be automatically corrected for spelling, usage, etc. But Lepper discovered that it did not contain the word "empathetic"!

In short, there are some, but few advances in the theory and assessment of conation to date. We had better push that research frontier to dovetail with the research in cognitive science or we may end up with instructional and assessment technology fit only for robots. Perhaps this is where the human teacher or tutor comes in again as a compensatory device.

Conclusion

Let me conclude with optimism. Imagine a combined instructional-assessment system that does all the good things mentioned here, and removes all the problems:

- It adapts its aptitude assessments to diagnose individual strengths on which the next instructional steps can build, while also alternating into aptitude-development training periodically to build up weaknesses.

- It adapts its achievement assessments to circumvent inaptitudes, while ascertaining the present state of the learner with respect to each instructional goal, both short-term and long-term.

- It chooses the form and content of the next instructional step based on these profiles and tailors the language and situational characteristics of this step to the interests and motivational states of the learner as well.

- It even guides the learner toward increased self-regulation as a learner.

- There is synchrony between technology and teacher, between macroadaptation and microadaptation, and between curriculum domains.

That would be quite a sight to see. And I think we have a chance to see it.

References

Ackerman, P. L. (1987). Individual differences in skill learning: An integration of psychometric and information processing perspectives. *Psychological Bulletin, 102,* 3-27.

Anderson, R. C., Shirey, L. L., Wilson, P. T., & Fielding, L. G. (1987). Interesting-ness of children's reading material. In R. E. Snow & M. J. Farr (Eds.), *Aptitude, learning, and instruction, Vol. 3: Conative and affective process analyses* (pp. 287-298). Hillsdale, NJ: Lawrence Erlbaum Associates.

Bethell-Fox, C. E., Lohman, D. F., & Snow, R. E. (1984). Adaptive reasoning: Componential and eye movement analysis of geometric analogy perfor-mance. *Intelligence, 8,* 205-238.

Brown, J. S., & Burton, R. R. (1978). Diagnostic models for procedural bugs in basic mathematical skills. *Cognitive Science, 2,* 155-192.

Brown, A. L., & Campione, J. C. (1986). Psychological theory and the study of learning disabilities. *American Psychologist, 41,* 1059-1068.

Brown, A. L., & Ferrara, R. A. (1985). Diagnosing zones of proximal development. In J. Wertsch (Ed.), *Culture, communication and cognition: Vygotskian perspectives* (pp. 273-305). Cambridge: Cambridge University Press.

Butterfield, E. C., Nielsen, D., Tangen, K. L., & Richardson, M. B. (1985). Theoretically-based psychometric measures of inductive reasoning. In S. E. Embretson (Ed.), *Test design: Developments in psychology and psychometrics* (pp. 77-148). Orlando, FL: Academic Press.

Calfee, R. C. (this volume). The teacher's role in using assessment to improve learning.

Campione, J. C., & Brown A. L. (1984). Learning ability and transfer propensity as sources of individual differences in intelligence. In P. H. Brooks, C. McCauley, & R. Sperber (Eds.), *Learning and cognition in the mentally retarded.* Hillsdale, NJ: Lawrence Erlbaum Associates.

Campione, J. C., Brown, A. L., Ferrara, R. A., Jones, R. S., & Sternberg, E. (1985). Breakdown in flexible use of information: Intelligence-related differences in transfer following equivalent learning performance. *Intelligence, 9,* 297-315.

Cronbach, L. J., & Snow, R. E. (1977). *Aptitudes and instructional methods: A handbook for research on interactions.* New York: Irvington.

Embretson, S. E. (1985). Multicomponent latent trait models for test design. In S. E. Embretson (Ed.), *Test design: Developments in psychology and psychometrics* (pp. 195-218). New York: Academic Press.

Ferrara, R. A., Brown, A. L., & Campione, J. C. (1986). Children's learning and transfer of inductive reasoning rules: Studies of proximal development. *Child Development, 57,* 1087-1099.

Frederiksen, J. R. (1981). Sources of process interaction in reading. In A. M. Lesgold & C. A. Perfetti (Eds.), *Interactive processes in reading* (pp. 361-386). Hillsdale, NJ: Lawrence Erlbaum Associates.

Frederiksen, J. R. (1982). A componential theory of reading skills and their interactions. In R. J. Sternberg (Ed.), *Advances in the psychology of human intelligence* (Vol. 1, pp. 125-180). Hillsdale, NJ: Lawrence Erlbaum Associates.

Frederiksen, J. R., Warren, B. M., & Roseberg, A. S. (1985a). A componential approach to training reading skills: Part 1. Perceptual units training. *Cognition and Instruction, 2,* 91-130.

Frederiksen, J. R., Warren, B. M., & Roseberg, A. S. (1985b). A componential approach to training reading skills: Part 2. Decoding and use of context. *Cognition and Instruction*, 2, 271-338.

Freeman, E. E. (Ed.). (1986). *The redesign of testing for the 21st century.* Proceedings of the 1985 ETS Invitational Conference. Princeton, NJ: Educational Testing Service.

Glaser, R. (1977). *Adaptive education: Individual diversity and learning.* New York: Holt, Rinehart & Winston.

Glaser, R., Lesgold, A., & Lajoie, S. (in press). Toward a cognitive theory for the measurement of achievement. In R. Ronning, J. Glover, J. C. Conoley, & J. W. H. Witt (Eds.), *The influence of cognitive psychology on testing and measurement: The Buros-Nebraska symposium on measurement and testing* (Vol. 3). Hillsdale, NJ: Lawrence Erlbaum Associates.

Gott, S. P. (this volume). Assessing technical expertise in today's work environments.

Greeno, J. G. (1986, April). Mathematical cognition: Accomplishments and challenges in research. Invited address to the American Educational Research Association, San Francisco.

Greeno, J. G., & Mayer, R. E. (1975). Structural and quantitative interaction among aptitudes and instructional treatments. Unpublished manuscript. Ann Arbor, MI: University of Michigan.

Holyoak, K. J. (1984). Analogical thinking and human intelligence. In R. J. Sternberg (Ed.), *Advances in the psychology of human intelligence* (Vol. 2, pp. 199-230). Hillsdale, NJ: Lawrence Erlbaum Associates.

Hunt, E., & Lansman, M. (1982). Individual differences in attention. In R. J. Sternberg (Ed.), *Advances in the psychology of human intelligence* (Vol. 1, pp. 207-254). Hillsdale, NJ: Lawrence Erlbaum Associates.

Kyllonen, P. C., Lohman, D. F., & Woltz, D. J. (1984). Componential modeling of alternative strategies for performing spatial tasks. *Journal of Educational Psychology, 76*, 1325-1345.

Lepper, M. R. (1987). Personal communication.

Lepper, M. R., & Malone, T. W. (1987). Intrinsic motivation and instructional effectiveness in computer-based education. In R. E. Snow & M. J. Farr (Eds.), *Aptitude, learning, and instruction, Vol. 3: Conative and affective process analyses* (pp. 255-283). Hillsdale, NJ: Lawrence Erlbaum Associates.

Lesgold, A. M. (this volume). The integration of instruction and assessment in technical jobs.

Lesgold, A. M., Bonar, J., & Ivill, J. (1987). *Toward intelligent systems for testing.* Technical Report Number LSP-1. Pittsburgh, PA: University of Pittsburgh, Learning Research and Development Center.

Lohman, D. F. (in press). Spatial abilities as traits, processes,and knowledge. In R. J. Sternberg (Ed.), *Advances in the psychology of human intelligence* (Vol. 4). Hillsdale, NJ: Lawrence Erlbaum Associates.

Malone, T. W., & Lepper, M. R. (1987). Making learning fun: A taxonomy of intrinsic motivations for learning. In R. E. Snow & M. J. Farr (Eds.), *Aptitude, learning, and instruction, Vol. 3: Conative and affective process analyses* (pp. 223-250). Hillsdale, NJ: Lawrence Erlbaum Associates.

Mislevy, R. J., & Verhelst, N. (1986). Modeling item responses when different subjects employ different solution strategies. Unpublished paper. Princeton, NJ: Educational Testing Service.

Novick, L. R. (1987). Analogical transfer in expert and novice problem solvers. Doctoral dissertation, Stanford University, 1986. *Dissertation Abstracts International, 47,* 3991B.

Pellegrino, J. W., & Glaser, R. (1979). Cognitive correlates and components in the analysis of individual differences. In R. J. Sternberg & D. K. Detterman (Eds.), *Human intelligence: Perspectives on its theory and measurement* (pp. 61-88). Norwood, NJ: Ablex.

Pellegrino, J. W., & Glaser, R. (1982). Analyzing aptitudes for learning: Inductive reasoning. In R. Glaser (Ed.), *Advances in instructional psychology* (Vol. 2, pp. 269-345). Hillsdale, NJ: Lawrence Erlbaum Associates.

Plake, B. S., & Witt, J. C. (Eds.) (1986). *The future of testing: The Buros-Nebraska symposium on measurement and testing* (Vol. 2). Hillsdale, NJ: Lawrence Erlbaum Associates.

Resnick, L. B. (1984). Beyond error analysis: The role of understanding in elementary school arithmetic. In H. N. Cheek (Ed.), *Diagnostic and prescriptive mathematics: Issues, ideas and insights.* 1984 Research Monograph (pp. 2-14). Kent, OH: Research Council for Diagnosis and Prescriptive Mathematics Research.

Ronning, R., Glover, J., Conoley, J. C., & Witt, J. W. H. (Eds.) (in press), *The influence of cognitive psychology on testing and measurement: The Buros-Nebraska symposium on measurement and testing* (Vol. 3). Hillsdale, NJ: Lawrence Erlbaum Associates.

Snow, R. E. (1980a). Aptitude, learner control, and adaptive instruction. *Educational Psychologist, 15,* 151-158.

Snow, R. E. (1980b). Aptitude and achievement. *New Directions for Testing and Measurement, 5*, 39-59.

Snow, R. E., & Farr, M. J. (1987). Cognitive-conative-affective processes in aptitude, learning, and instruction: An introduction. In R. E. Snow & M. J. Farr (Eds.), *Aptitude, learning, and instruction, Vol. 3: Conative and affective process analyses* (pp. 1-8). Hillsdale, NJ: Lawrence Erlbaum Associates.

Snow, R. E., & Lohman, D. F. (1984). Toward a theory of cognitive aptitude for learning from instruction. *Journal of Educational Psychology, 76*, 347-376.

Snow, R. E., & Lohman, D. F. (in press). Implications of cognitive psychology for educational measurement. In R. L. Linn (Ed.), *Educational measurement*. New York: Macmillan.

Sternberg, R. J. (Ed.) (1985). *Human abilities: An information processing approach.* New York: W. H. Freeman & Co..

Wang, M. C. (this volume). The wedding of instruction and assessment in the classroom.

Testing in the Service of Learning Science: Learning-Assessment Systems That Promote Educational Excellence and Equality

JOSEPH I. LIPSON
Professor of Communication Design
California State University, Chico

Current trends in cognitive science, information technology, and testing suggest that we can develop mastery tests in science that can avoid some of the probable negative side-effects of present testing procedures and encourage more effective teaching and learning practices. The research and development needed to reach these goals promises to be difficult, but if we succeed, the contribution of enhanced testing methods will justify the effort many times over.

The following is a brief overview of the points I would like to make to support my argument:

1. I will address the influence of **mastery tests in science** and the role of **advanced computer technology** in developing and delivering such tests.

2. The idea of mastery, as I will use it, is related to the idea of **expertise** in a domain and skills mastered to the point that they have become **automatic.** These mastery tests should identify and recognize strengths as well as identify and help students to manage their misconceptions in science. The reason for this is that in a wide range of situations it has been found that capitalizing on strength and managing weakness are the key to optimizing human productivity.

3. An important point in considering the influence of mastery tests as compared to present-day tests is that **anticipation of a test and a test format** influences both **conscious and unconscious decisions** that affect what and how we learn. Mastery tests should improve learning

and teaching by providing more appropriate goals, by encouraging practice, by recognizing what has been learned outside the formal curriculum, and by challenging the student to reach for higher levels of knowledge and skill. In other words, if we test for mastery, we are likely to get teaching and learning for mastery.

4. Evidence suggests that present-day multiple-choice tests have important **limitations** in the kinds of items they can present.

5. The emerging generation of **computer and information technology** is capable of building mastery tests. In addition, this technology can provide **maps** of knowledge and skill that result from testing in scientific and applied contexts. With this overview, I will discuss the need for mastery tests in more detail.

Although many of the arguments I will use have implications for testing in other domains, I will address the application of mastery tests to science education—education for learning concepts, heuristics, and applications. There is considerable evidence that we, as a nation, do not do well in science. Only about eight percent of our students take a high-school course in physics, and we do not compare well to other industrialized nations in tests of math and science. In a world increasingly based on science and related technologies, this weakness is serious both for individuals and society as a whole, and for minorities and women in particular.

As we know, tests serve many important functions. I want to discuss two effects: results and anticipation. Results effects, which involve information about what a student knows and does not know, can make instruction more effective and efficient. Reports using aggregated information can identify students for remediation and tracking, as well as for gatekeeping. Test results generate research data and are used for planning, monitoring teacher and school performance, allocating resources, and ensuring educational opportunity, instructional quality, and educational equity (Goertz, 1986). Test results can also provide important input for state and national educational policy decisions (Messick, 1986).

"Anticipation effects" refers to the effects that knowing one is going to be tested (as well as knowing the content and format of the anticipated test) have on teaching and learning. I want to look more closely at these anticipation effects.

A commonly noted and fairly obvious interaction between testing and learning is that teachers and systems often teach to the test. This is not too surprising (Tyler & White, 1979). The implication is that, if we modify our tests, we will almost certainly modify how students and teachers spend their time and effort. Knowledge of how we are to be tested affects conscious decisions regarding how we study, allocate our attention, organize our knowledge, and spend our learning time and effort (Frederiksen, 1984).

The second influence of test anticipation on learning is much less frequently noted; only a few relevant studies have come to our attention (Balota & Neely, 1980). I would state this less frequently noted influence as follows: **Knowledge of how we are to be tested alters how we subconsciously process information and organize knowledge in our minds.**

While my reasoning can be inferred from recent findings on subconscious or unconscious processing (Kihlstrom, 1987), the point is made most directly in a study (Foos & Clark, 1984) which reported the following results (Camer, 1984):

Students were told to expect an essay, multiple-choice, "memory," or some unspecified type of test. In fact, everyone took the same test, which included multiple-choice and short-answer items and asked students to list the best and worst countries on human rights. The results revealed that "... students expecting a multiple-choice test scored lowest, *even on the multiple-choice items*." (Emphasis mine.)

"One could reason that students who studied for a multiple-choice test might have keyed on facts, not concepts. But this would not explain why those expecting an essay did better *even on the multiple-choice items*." (Emphasis mine.)

This evidence once again suggests that if we seek teaching and learning for mastery, we should test for mastery.

Limitations of current tests

Current formal tests such as those administered on a large scale in our schools and colleges have several limitations:

1. **Items tend to be independent of a common subject context.**

Sequences of test items are usually not related to each other in any systematic way. As a result, current tests do not require the performance that is really desired. A person cannot display, in a realistic context, all he or she knows about a domain being tested. Such items usually do not require a student to integrate an array of knowledge and skill.

The consequence may be a payoff for the acquisition of fragmented, unconnected, quickly forgotten knowledge that is not the kind needed to solve a long-term problem, conduct an extended experiment, or execute a design task. A fragmented set of items is in contrast to a struggle for mastery in which one learns, organizes, and applies knowledge and skill in a specific domain. Consider, for example, the way one organizes knowledge for a lecture or thinks through how to explain a laboratory procedure to a classmate. These comments suggest that tests in which the student is confronted with realistic situations will prepare students to master those kinds of situations (Frederiksen, 1984).

2. **Items do not use dynamic images and do not make extensive use of photographs.**

At least partly because of the limitations of our current testing technology, our items are heavily oriented toward verbally stated items. These are not truly representative of a scientist's knowledge. Much scientific knowledge involves understanding of dynamic processes and procedures that take place in time. Also, science refers to phenomena that are inherently visual and dynamic (Greenfield, 1986). This suggests the desirability of test items that could present the student with a rich array of pictures or dynamic presentations, ask the student to select the correct photograph or dynamic sequence, or ask the student to identify an error in a dynamic sequence.

3. **Items do not adequately take account of the interests, goals, and instructional and other learning experiences of the student being tested.**

Especially in the field of science and related technologies, a student may know much more outside of the school curriculum than within it. For example, many students become quite expert in computer technology and programming, even when this is absent from the school curriculum. This point is not made to lessen the importance of the school curriculum. Rather, it is to suggest that we can enhance formal education by tests that recognize, value, and exploit knowledge and skill wherever they have been acquired.

4. **Formal tests tend to reflect a subtle cultural bias, an issue that directly affects equality.**

I am concerned with more than referents that may be unfamiliar to the student. I am more concerned with: (a) the cultural values that may determine that one kind of test or test item is better able to command the student's attention than another; (b) the way information-processing in the minds of students may vary, so that one form of item is more confusing than another; and (c) the way that forms of testing and the testing environment may affect members of a particular culture. I am concerned here with the cultural world-view, perspective, preferences, intentions, and goals that influence test performance. In short, I would like to use what we know about cultural effects to design tests that adjust to the cultural orientation of students in order to get the best out of all our students.

What is mastery?

Mastery involves the following (Glaser, 1986):

- A fund of knowledge of the scientific domain—laws, facts, principles, examples, and applications.

- Automated skills such as lab procedures, problem solving, experimental design, troubleshooting.

- Talent in seeing patterns, asking the right question, following an anomalous result, constructing apparatus, inventing a new approach or technique.

- Aesthetic sense of what is beautiful in the discipline.

- Interplay between declarative knowledge and procedural knowledge. The expert uses his or her knowledge to orchestrate components of automated skill.

- Usually an expert is sought out for help or advice. However, the best performer is often not the best coach or teacher.

- Mastery also requires practice, practice, practice. Therefore, mastery tests imply the opportunity to practice.

If the above are the general characteristics of mastery in a domain, what is special about science?

31

Science poses special problems for mastery testing. The range of disciplines is great, and the differences between disciplines evoke very different definitions of what knowledge and skill are important. The test items, if they are to be realistic representations of mastery, must reflect these domain differences. Each scientific discipline has its own special vocabulary, its own use of symbols and mathematics, its own class of problems and design tasks. As noted, science testing, more than most other areas of study, will benefit from access to animation, motion pictures of techniques and natural processes, and simulations of natural and laboratory events.

The scoring and scaling of mastery tests in science will be challenging. A beginning student will need to see progress that may seem trivial to a science buff; the knowledge of two different Westinghouse Scholarship finalists may be impressive while scarcely overlapping. Finally, to avoid traumatizing students, the mastery test should have qualities that encourage, invite, interest, and appeal at the same time that it challenges.

If we accept that mastery tests are a promising approach to excellence and equality and that current tests can't do the job, what direction should we take? It is my judgment that modern information technology offers a solution. We can create mastery tests that largely compensate for the limitations of current standardized tests. The evidence for this lies in expert judgment and examples of existing software.

The generation of computers just becoming available and those that will be developed in the next five years appear to make new kinds of mastery testing feasible. Each of the following capabilities is in contrast to present limitations:

1. **We can ensure that declarative and procedural knowledge and verbal and nonverbal representations are assessed.**

For example, using animation and/or sequences on a videodisc, we can probe a student's concepts and misconceptions in science. We might have an animated display of various trajectories for an object thrown horizontally from a cliff and ask the student to select which trajectory is correct. We can show motion pictures of processes and procedures and ask the student to touch the screen or press a key the instant an error is detected.

2. **We can include student choice of domain, style, starting point.**

With a sufficiently large bank of items stored in the computer, we can give the student the option of domain, style of questions, and starting level of difficulty. For example, a student who is interested in cooking may feel more comfortable with science questions that use the chemistry and physics of the kitchen as their context. A student whose hobby is ham radio may select this as the domain for initial testing. A student who is insecure may ask for an easy starting point. Computer-adaptive testing can adjust the rate at which questions become more challenging.

3. **We can react to student preferences, personality, past and present performance.**

The computer can gradually build, store, and display a map of student preferences, interests, and past performance. We can determine whether a student is interested in a particular aspect of science, such as the history of science, or a particular kind of activity (e.g., dissecting animals, conducting plant experiments, building devices, troubleshooting and fixing equipment, solving puzzles, writing computer programs). This information can be supplied to the student, teachers, and parents to be used in grouping students with similar interests, recommending activities and books, and selecting test items that key into the student's existing knowledge.

4. **We can supply construction toolboxes.**

There are many simulation programs that have been developed in recent years. Programs such as *Chipwitz, Rocky's Boots, Robot Odyssey, Stella*, and *Thinglab* suggest that we can give the student a toolbox and a box of components to build and test devices. For example, a beginning student of electricity could build on the computer screen a simple circuit to power a light bulb or an electromagnetic relay. A more advanced student could build an electric doorbell, a radio receiver, or a logic circuit.

5. **We can generate a map of the student's knowledge.**

As the student's interaction with the mastery tests accumulates, we should be able to display—for the student, teacher, and others—a two-dimensional graphic display or map that conveys his or her growing knowledge and competence and that defines the boundary between what the student knows and does not know. This map can challenge the student to practice and learn what is needed to move to higher levels of mastery.

Conclusion

Science education is one of the foundations of our health as a society. Testing influences almost every aspect of the educational enterprise in a variety of ways. Our present mass-testing system is itself a product of information technology. The rapid advances in information technology offer us opportunities to apply new intellectual tools to the development and delivery of tests that more closely reflect the kinds of performance our students will find in life. Society and our children can realize the benefits if you and the organizations you represent become committed to the task.

References

Balota, D. A., & Neely, J. H. (1980). Test-expectancy and word-frequency effects in recall and recognition. *Journal of Experimental Psychology: Human Learning and Memory, 6(5),* 576-587.

Bunderson, C. V., Inouye, D. K., & Olsen, J. B. (in press). The four generations of computerized educational measurement.

Caramazza, A., McCloskey, M., & Green, B. F. (1981). Naive beliefs in 'sophisticated' subjects: Misconceptions about trajectories of objects. *Cognition, 9,* 117-123.

Frederiksen, N. (March 1984). The real test bias: Influences of testing on teaching and learning. *American Psychologist, 39(3),* 193-202.

Glaser, R. (1986). Intelligence as acquired proficiency. In R. J. Sternberg & D. K. Detterman (Eds.), *What is intelligence?* Norwood, NJ: Ablex.

Goertz, M. E. (January 1986). State educational standards: a 50-state survey. Research Report. Princeton, NJ: Educational Testing Service.

Green, B. F., McCloskey, M., & Caramazza, A. (October 1980). The relation of knowledge to problem solving with examples from kinematics. Talk presented at NIE-LRDC Conference on Thinking and Learning Skills, Pittsburgh.

Greenfield, P. M. (1986). Electronic technologies, education, and cognitive development. In D. E. Berger, K. Pezdek, & W. P. Banks (Eds.), *Applications of cognitive psychology: Problem solving, education, and computing.* Hillsdale, NJ: Lawrence Erlbaum Associates.

Kihlstrom, J. F. (September 1987). The cognitive unconscious. *Science, 237,* 1445-1451.

Lesgold, A. M. (1984). Acquiring expertise. In J. R. Anderson & S. M. Kosslyn (Eds.), *Tutorials in learning and memory*. San Francisco: W. H. Freeman & Co.

McCloskey, M., & Kohl, D. (1983). Naive physics: The curvilinear impulse principle and its role in interactions with moving objects. *Journal of Experimental Psychology: Learning Memory and Cognition, 9(1)*, 146-156.

Messick, S. (1986). Large-scale educational assessment as policy research: Aspirations and limitations. Research Report. Princeton, NJ: Educational Testing Service.

Minstrell, J., & Smith, C. (January 1982). Explaining the 'at rest' condition of an object. *The Physics Teacher*.

Munday, L. A., & Davis, J. Varieties of accomplishment after college: Perspectives on the meaning of academic talent. Research Report Series #62. Iowa City, Iowa: American College Testing.

Schwartz, J. L. (1979?) Project TORQUE—pieces of a paper. Internal document. Boston: Massachusetts Institute of Technology, Division for Study and Research in Education.

Schwartz, J. L. (no date). What is measurable? *The Times Educational Supplement*.

Tyler, R. W., & White, S. H. (October 1979). *Testing, teaching and learning: Report of a conference on research on testing*. Washington, DC: National Institute of Education.

Zacharias, J. R. (October 1979). The sciences and technologies. In R. W. Tyler & S. H. White (Eds.), *Testing, teaching and learning: Report of a conference on research on testing*. Washington, DC: National Institute of Education.

Cognitive and Environmental Perspectives on Assessing Achievement

ROBERT GLASER
University Professor of Psychology and Education and
Director, Learning Research and Development Center
University of Pittsburgh

Two perspectives, at least, must work together if advances in assessment are to serve learning. Snow and Lipson have spoken well to the cognitive perspective, as was their mandate. In addition, I want to raise some concerns about perceptions of and approaches to testing—to offer a second perspective that I call the environmental perspective. If the advances in the study of cognition are to be well utilized, they must mesh with and help generate a testing environment where definitions of achievement that will support future performance are taken into account.

The cognitive perspective

First, let me present some thoughts on the cognitive perspective. It is now well recognized that advances in the understanding of human cognition can enable us to focus more precisely than ever before on the complex processes that underlie school achievement—a focus that emphasizes the structure and coherence of knowledge and its accessibility in problem solving and reasoning.

Cognitive studies investigate how knowledge is organized, how problems are represented for solution, and how mental models are imposed on the interpretation of information; in short, they have begun to reveal how competence in a subject matter develops with the acquisition of facts and propositions and is further heightened with the flexible use of this knowledge under varied conditions and goals.

The analysis of performance is making explicit the outcomes of learning and experience that can be assessed to guide the further acquisition of knowledge and skill in various domains. We are better able now to describe the stages of competence or levels of achievement that underlie the progressions of learning within a domain of knowledge, and, in more effective ways, to foster the transition to higher levels of competence through appropriately designed instruction.

Given the growth of this research, we should be in a position to consider cognitive-psychological theory as well as psychometric theory in the design of tests. To date, we have been primarily reaping the benefits of psychometrics, employing advances in statistical theory, but have had less opportunity to utilize cognitive and developmental theory that explicates human thinking and performance. This pattern of research use has meant that most of the work of testing technology—the analysis of item difficulty, discrimination indices, scaling and norming procedures, and the analysis of factorial composition—has occurred after test items were constructed.

In the future, test design will entail extensive attention to theory before and during item design as well. As we also reap the benefits of research on human performance and development, we will rely on the emerging picture of the properties of acquired proficiency in the learning of school subjects, thereby making testing responsive to the structures and processes that develop as individuals move from beginning to advanced learners. Thus, the assessment of achievement can be more closely tied to our understanding of progressions in learning and the accrual of results of effective teaching.

Indicators of developing competence

Essential characteristics of complex performances have been described in the various domains of mathematics, science, social science, reading, and writing. These characteristics provide useful indices of the acquisition of competence. We know that, at successive stages of learning, there exist different integrations of knowledge, different forms of skill, and differences in the rapidity of access to knowledge and in the efficiency of performance—all of which contribute to different levels of achievement. These properties, some of which have been described by Snow and Lipson, can define criteria for test design. As competence in a subject matter grows, performance becomes more coherent and more principled, more useful, efficient, and self-regulatory. These qualities are each a candidate dimension for the assessment of achievement.

The coherence of knowledge. As competence is attained, elements of knowledge become more interconnected so that proficient individuals access coherent chunks of information rather than fragments. Beginners' knowledge is spotty, consisting of isolated definitions and superficial understandings. As proficiency develops, these items of information become structured and are integrated with past organizations of knowledge so that they are retrieved from memory in larger units. Thus, structuredness, coherence, and accessibility to interrelated chunks of knowledge become targets for assessment and objectives for instruction.

Principled problem solving. Certain forms of problem interpretation are correlated with the ability to carry out the details of a task or the steps of a problem solution. Novices work on the basis of problem representations that rely on the surface feature of a task situation or problem; in contrast, more proficient individuals identify principles that lie beneath apparent surface features as they represent a problem. Ability for fast recognition and perception of underlying principles and patterns is an indication of developing competence that could be assessed by appropriate test tasks in verbal and graphic situations.

Usable knowledge. As Lipson pointed out, studies of expert-novice differences suggest that the course of knowledge acquisition proceeds from the accumulation of facts in declarative or propositional form to their compilation in condition-action form. Novices can know a principle, a rule, or a specialized vocabulary without knowing the conditions where that knowledge applies and how it can be used most effectively. When knowledge is accessed by experts, it is bound to conditions of applicability. Experts and novices may be equally competent at recalling specific items of information, but the experts relate these items to the goals of problem solution and conditions for action. The progression from declarative to procedural and goal-oriented information is a significant dimension of assessment in acquiring competence in an area of knowledge.

Attention-free and efficient performance. In many situations, experts' performances are distinguished by a speed that is remarkable, given the limits in human ability to deal with competing attention-demanding tasks. This speed is, to a great extent, attributable to effective interaction between the basic and advanced components of performance that need to be integrated as skill is acquired.

In such domains as text comprehension and medical diagnosis, as in tennis, attention must alternate between basic skills and higher levels of strategy; thus, automaticity in basic component skills is crucial to quick and effective performance. Moreover, although basic automatic and attention-demanding component processes may work well when taught and tested separately, for competent performance, they must be developed so they work together smoothly. In instruction aimed at the development of higher levels of proficiency, basic component skills should be automatized—made attention-free—so that conscious thought can be devoted to aspects of performance where it is indispensable.

A dimension of competence, then, is the efficiency of subprocesses required for minimal interference with conscious thought; these subprocesses must have progressed to a point where they facilitate and are integrated into total performance.

Self-regulatory skills. With accruing competence, people develop skills for monitoring their performance. They are good at apportioning their time, asking questions about what they have to do, assessing the relevance of their knowledge, and predicting the outcomes of their efforts. They rapidly check their problem solutions, and they are more accurate at judging problem difficulty. These self-regulatory skills are less developed in individuals with performance difficulties. Because they are used to oversee its use, they enhance knowledge. Thus, they are important candidates for assessment and instruction, and they can be significant predictors of an individual's problem-solving abilities.

Environmental perspective

Consider now the necessary coordinate environmental perspective. New uses of tests will not occur unless the testing environment and the attitudes of the administrators and recipients of tests are in tune with goals now accessible to us. In this regard, I consider three attitudes crucial: (1) We should view tests as assessments of enablement, (2) we must realize that tests dictate and enforce norms, and (3) we should keep in mind that tests can preclude judgment and action.

Enabling competences. To place tests in the service of learning, we must foster an environment in which assessments of school subject matter are seen as measures of those skills and dispositions that are essential to future learning rather than merely of past achievement. Once mastered, the skills and knowledge of a domain can become enabling competencies for the future. With this in mind, we must measure student attainment in a way that takes into account, for example, that the purpose of students learning to read is to enable them to learn from reading. Addressing reading as an enabling skill implies a particular environment for achievement whereby the command of reading becomes sufficiently automatic that the student can concentrate on analyzing or interpreting the meaning of the text or concept. This concern with enablement raises the level of competence that we should measure and that schools should be held accountable for.

The same is the case for writing, which, as an enabling skill, provides a way of organizing as well as communicating thought. Those who cannot express thoughts in writing are clearly at a great disadvantage in both school and work, so that the standard of assessment should go beyond mechanics and involve the ability to use writing to help clarify ideas and build persuasive arguments. This holds true for other school subject matter including the natural and social sciences. We must assess the ability to think critically about our physical and social worlds—to formulate questions and seek answers.

This attitude of enablement should motivate us to assess knowledge in terms of its constructive use for further learning. Knowledge at every level would be assessed to allow us to determine whether students can use their current achievements to gather further information, evaluate evidence, weigh alternative courses for action, and articulate reasoned arguments. Thus, tests would reinforce the view that these attainments should be an integral part of learning the traditional subject areas of schooling.

Enforcement of norms. A second concern of this environmental perspective is the feedback of tests to teaching and learning—put more strongly, the power of tests in setting standards and norms. It is quite clear that human beings rise to the requirements of their circumstances. In times of emergency and stress, we are capable of doing more than we think we can do, and also, in times of low demands, doing less than we can do. Environmental demands not only elicit exceptional and lesser performances, they also establish norms. This setting of norms is a critical consequence of tests. When we test at one level, that level becomes a norm for aspiration; when we test at another level, a new norm is established, and we teach and learn to that level.

Often tests assess small, disparate items of knowledge; this is a disservice to learning because knowledge becomes increasingly connected and principled as competence is attained. We know that proficient students think in terms of coherent units of information rather than fragments, so that it is significant to test the ability to make inferences on the bases of interrelated information and integrated sequences of performance. Tests must be designed to require these significant aspects of accomplishment.

Another aspect of proficiency for which tests should set a standard is knowledge of the conditions where facts and principles apply and are used most effectively. With the growth of competence, knowledge becomes more functional -- it is tied to conditions of use and to the accomplishment of goals of reasoning. Thus, to test the reaches of attained knowledge, we must determine whether the learner has acquired not only the crucial facts and concepts but also the conditions for their adaptive use. Unless we do so, we test only to the knowledge of the beginner and not to the mature use of knowledge.

The obvious merits repeating. Testing practices establish norms of performance that enhance or depress the aspirations and accomplishments of students and teachers. Unless we closely attend to the direction of its influence, assessment can be a major *disservice* to learning.

Preclusion of judgment. The impact of tests in the service of learning is evident particularly where a test result becomes more than a tool for placing students in a category. A test result's function should not end with a classification that precludes judgment by the teacher and student about paths of action. Measurement in other fields, like medical diagnosis, results in an action—a prescription, a therapeutic exercise.

Too often we consider assessment complete when we place students at a grade level or percentile. Such testing practice can persuade us that we have made an educational decision to assist the learner, although we have not. Assessments can produce valuable information and should be designed so that alternative actions and instructional possibilities are apparent.

Finally, I wish to compliment Snow and Lipson for contributions that have helped make us aware of advances in cognitive science that can assist with the design of new forms of assessment. Test developers and educators are beginning to examine the benefits to educational practice that our expanding knowledge of learning can afford. It remains to be seen, however, whether the contemporary concern with improvement in education and training will encourage both technical change and the testing environment that can allow us to secure full benefit of scientific advances.

The Teacher's Role in Using Assessment to Improve Learning

Robert Calfee
Stanford University
and
Elfrieda Hiebert
University of Colorado

Our thesis in this paper is that the knowledgeable teacher plays a critical role in valid classroom assessment, and that effective instruction requires informed professional judgment. Our focus will be on the elementary grades and the curriculum of literacy. Prevailing practice finds the teacher's discernment displaced by externally mandated tests and test-like instruments of limited depth and scope (Calfee & Drum, 1979; Haertel & Calfee, 1983; Cole, this volume), conditions that undercut the teacher's professional role. Pre-service preparation and the school work-place both steer teachers toward the role of "meter readers."

This situation reflects a distrust of teachers' capacity to be objective in assessing student achievement, hence the efforts to "automate" the task. Such a strategy may work when a low-level definition of literacy fits policy needs. For modern times and in democratic societies, however, an important goal of schooling is the development of individual autonomy:

> the centerpiece of education [is] empowering our children in the use of the written and the spoken word so they can be personally empowered and civically engaged . . .
>
> (Boyer, 1986; also Strike, 1982)

This goal envisions teachers who are personally and professionally empowered, who are capable of making informed and trustworthy judgments. It means that "teachers must make decisions, they must provide guidance, they must set standards of accomplishment . . . they must wear the mantle of professionalism" (Ravitch, 1984, p. 66). This description applies to relatively few reading teachers in today's elementary classrooms. Youngsters from at-risk backgrounds are especially likely to encounter mechanistic, worksheet-driven instruction.

Our paper begins by *contrasting the present state of affairs with the situation 50 years ago.* We do not mean to portray a "golden age," but to remember a time when teachers were more autonomous and more reliant on their own judgment in assessing students. This contrast leads us to ask: *What is literacy and how should it be assessed by the classroom teacher?*

The answers to both of these questions, we will argue, are policy dependent. If schools are to help all youngsters attain the level of literacy they need to participate in a modern, democratic society, then *teachers must become "researchers."* Assessment becomes research methodology, rather than testing for selection.

The next section reviews *current realities:* What are elementary teachers taught about assessment during pre-service training? What do they appear to know and do in the classroom? The paper ends with summary *recommendations.*

Two snapshots

Mrs. Aiken: Reflections of the first author.

Spring of 1943, Durham, North Carolina—Mrs. Aiken had learned a lot about her third graders during the past eight months. Though we thought she was omniscient, she was actually a skilled observer, with care to design activities that informed her. We had to "read with meaning," we had to "show our work" in arithmetic; getting the right answer wasn't the only thing, and we had to write a lot.

Fridays were test days—"Put your books in the desk, and take out a blank piece of paper. Make sure your pencil is sharp." Mrs. Aiken had selected words to spell, sentences to correct, questions to answer from the story we studied earlier in the week. She returned the tests on Monday; we took them home to our parents. The scores recorded in the grade book eventually took shape as A's and B's. We got a grade for deportment. Third grade was important to me. By year's end I had learned a lot, and knew that I could do well in school.

Today's teacher:

Mrs. Aiken seemed to know what she was doing—perhaps the impression of an impressionistic third grader. Surveys suggest that today's teachers are less certain about their status as professionals. For instance, hear the thoughts of an elementary teacher as reported by Fraatz (1987):

"I wonder if we ever teach reading. Because reading is so complicated, and it's not complicated, that sometimes I don't know what I'm doing ... I don't know what reading is, after all these years, after a master's degree in reading ... I'm just a person that gives [the students] ways to approach something, just hoping it all fits together." (p. 7)

Many of Fraatz's interviews have this tone. The same pattern—an inarticulateness, an absence of professional status, a sense of routine, a feeling of isolation and loneliness—is reported by other observers (e.g., Jackson, 1968; Shulman, 1986). It is more frequent at the elementary level and in the basic skills. The portrayal by Chambliss (1986) of the assessment practices of a high school photography teacher is reminiscent of Mrs. Aiken. The teacher was quite explicit about goals, and the "final exam" was an exhibition.

When Fraatz's respondents discuss assessment, two themes appear: reading consists of the mastery of a complex array of low-level skills tested by the basal system, but school success (including reading achievement) also depends on social accommodation to the classroom as judged by the teacher:

"When I get test results, I write up a list of exactly what each child got wrong. . . . This might mean working on commas, alphabetizing, or silent consonants." (p. 37)

"[The children are] tested and everything, but that doesn't tell you that much. . . . When I see a kid on the floor, or he's talking or out of his seat, that's a sure hint that he doesn't know what he's doing. . . ." (p. 20)

Whether teachers focus on "skills" or social behavior, a recurring undertone is the limited impact of instruction; some students enter school with academic potential and family support, and others do not. The teacher's job is to manage the identification of student potential, the placement into groups according to ability, and the orderly movement of groups through content appropriate to their potential. The process is somewhat mysterious (Anyon, 1981):

"Professional uncertainty ... permeates both the assessment of reading needs and the provision of reading instruction . . ." (p. 29)

"The language teachers use to describe the needs and abilities of their students grows out of the materials the children use and the rate at which they are instructed . . ." (p. 50)

In summary, the teacher's core work depends today on external forces. Basal readers determine the curriculum objectives and pedagogical methods, worksheets direct student activities, and standardized tests are the final measure of success and failure. Greater external control has not enhanced either teacher confidence or public respect.

A contemporary vision of the literate person

You know about reading. The test is that you have made it this far in the document. On the other hand, to be competent in an area does not mean that one is expert, nor that one understands the area, nor that one can teach others. Educators should be especially fluent in articulating their profession, but the evidence suggests otherwise (Calfee, 1987b; Shulman, 1986; Piaget, 1970). The point is poignantly evident in the earlier comment, "I don't know what reading is, after all these years, after a master's degree in reading . . ." We will argue in this paper that it is critical for teachers to have a coherent and clearly articulated vision of a curriculum of literacy appropriate to our time and our society, a vision that integrates reading and writing and spoken language.

Literacy as an intellectual domain. So what is reading? The commonsense answer is clear enough: the skill of understanding a printed message. Unlike mathematics or science, literacy has no obvious disciplinary or university base. The reading teacher therefore faces a double whammy. As for most teachers, outsiders have little appreciation of the professional knowledge and skill needed to lead students to mastery of a domain. In addition, reading is not even recognized as a field of scholarship. The problem is especially acute for elementary teachers, who are not seen as expert in any subject matter, and so are frequently viewed as semiprofessionals. Their role is to teach the "basic skills"—reading, writing, and arithmetic. Everyone knows these areas, and so the task requires no specialized knowledge. Right?

Wrong! In fact, we would argue that elementary teachers, to meet the challenge of contemporary schooling, must attain a level of professional knowledge and expertise greater than most other educators and professionals in many other disciplines. The technological core of professional knowledge for the elementary teacher encompasses three domains—*curriculum, instruction*, and *assessment*. To be sure, the teacher's job has other significant facets, ranging from the sublime to the ridiculous, from understanding the social-emotional needs of children to handling classroom management (Calfee & Shefelbine, 1981), but the triplet listed above is central. Of these, curriculum is most critical. Instruction and assessment lack purpose until the goals are clearly articulated.

Curriculum encompasses the substance of a domain. While often confused with materials and activities, at its core it comprises a set of foundational ideas. Instruction is the delivery system, the actions of the teacher for implementing the curriculum. The aim is to provide students with opportunities to achieve independent mastery of concepts and skills. Assessment is the gathering of evidence to guide decisions about curriculum and instruction, and to evaluate the outcomes of instruction.

The curriculum of literacy. As noted, the substance of the elementary reading curriculum may seem obvious and even trivial to a "reader"; the task is simply for students to acquire fluency in translating print to sound. Once this basic goal is achieved, then the student can move from "learning to read" to "reading to learn" (Chall, 1983). Reading is *skill development* more than *intellectual growth*. Practice with feedback is a suitable instructional strategy. Assessment is immediate and direct—simply ask the student to read aloud.

This view of reading is adequate for certain purposes. Scribner and Cole (1978) describe literacy among the Vai tribe as the functional use of print for record-keeping and personal messages ("Having a wedding on Monday. Please come. RSVP. Joe"). In fact, the purposes of literacy span a continuum from "reading and writing your name" to mastery of the rhetoric as a tool for thinking and for communication. As Heath (1983), Olson (1977), Goody (1977), and others have noted, the upper levels of literacy bring significant shifts in language use: greater explicitness, more reliance on expository forms, fuller elaboration of arguments, less dependence on "Ya' know what I mean . . . "

"Ya' know" won't get you very far in today's world. A functional, practice-based vision of literacy is inadequate for survival in modern society. Success requires fully elaborated ability in the use of language. Elsewhere we have referred to this as the contrast between the *natural* and *formal* styles of language (Calfee & Drum, 1986). The distinction mirrors *spoken* versus *printed* forms of language, but the manner of use rather than the mode is the central goal. A "basic skills" definition of reading is inadequate for the individual and dangerous for the country. Policy makers (Jennings, 1986) have identified the "Sputnik of the Eighties" not as a dramatic challenge in space, but the slow and steady undermining of intellectual capital. Youngsters who did not finish school 50 years ago could still support the society and themselves. Jobs of the future require the informed use of "mind aids for the post-industrial knowledge-worker" (Feigenbaum & McCorduck, 1984). These demands touch virtually every individual; the IRS W-4 plagued all of us.

And so the new vision of the literate person takes shape as an individual with total command of language, whether printed or spoken. Moreover, the individual is articulate. He or she can explain the reasoning behind a problem, both the analysis of the issue and the strategy behind that analysis. The student must acquire this competence in the early stages of schooling; "Language is not just another subject; it is the means by which other subjects are pursued" (Boyer, 1986).

The elementary teacher, to guide youngsters toward achievement of this challenging goal, must know the building blocks of *linguistics* and *rhetoric* (Calfee & Drum, 1986). Unfortunately for Fraatz's teacher, these building blocks are not part of the professional development of today's teachers. Mrs. Aiken probably attended a "normal school," where she studied these topics as a matter of course. The textbook terms that have replaced these fundamental concepts are piecemeal and lack coherence. Teachers are honest in expressing confusion and uncertainty about the complexities of reading. They are undoubtedly literate, but lack the principled *structure of knowledge* (Wilson, Shulman, & Richert, 1987) that allows independent planning and decision-making. Enhanced understanding of teacher assessment begins with a clearer conceptualization of the curriculum, but let us move on.

Classroom assessment: routine or research

Classroom assessment in the elementary grades is often routinized and procedural. Students have to be assigned to ability groups at the beginning of the year, and so the teacher gives placement tests. The "robins" have finished Unit 6, and so they take the end-of-unit test. The child who fails a skill does additional worksheets until mastery (i.e., passing the test). It's time to fill out grade cards, and so the teacher checks students' progress in the basal materials and the curriculum tests. At the end of the school year, students take the district's standardized tests. The scores will not be ready until summer, but will be used for student placement in the fall.

Assessment under these conditions can resemble a team of workers sorting and grading apples. Some fruits are bigger and better than others, and the task is to classify and label. We have described an alternative model (Hiebert & Calfee, in press), in which the teacher is an *applied researcher*. The teacher in this model acts as an experimenter, searching for the conditions that promote student understanding and competence.

The investigation of a research question is far from routine. The first task is to formulate the problem and associated *hypotheses*. You must be clear about your goals. Second is creation of a *design*, a plan for systematic variation in factors thought to influence the phenomenon being investigated. Third is the task of *data collection*, the compiling and documentation of evidence. The fourth task is the *interpretation* of the data—what do the findings mean, what are alternative interpretations, how might the original hypotheses be reformulated to reflect the results? The process is not linear but interactive and cyclic, not a sequence of stages but a set of distinctive processes. Research flows in an iterative fashion rather than "proving" a point.

Data collection—testing—is no longer an end in itself, but serves a broader purpose. Reliability and validity are not statistics but approaches to the evaluation of evidence: Is the evidence internally consistent? Does it provide a trustworthy base for interpretation? Data on student performance are not for placement and selection, but are opportunities for reflection and experimentation.

What are teachers taught about reading assessment?

The model of classroom assessment sketched above does not "come naturally." It requires a blend of conceptual analysis with clinical wisdom. In this section we look at teachers' opportunities during pre-service education to acquire the necessary knowledge and skill. Our data base is an informal survey of textbooks in *educational psychology* and *reading instruction*. We would prefer to rely on a research literature, but the topic of teacher assessment has not attracted much attention. An ERIC search was unproductive; the *Third Handbook of Research on Teaching* (Wittrock, 1986) does not address the issue, and the *International Encyclopedia of Education* (Husen & Postlethwaite, 1985) has few points of reference.

The most helpful source we have found is Stiggins, Conklin, and Bridgeford (1986). The latter present a review of textbooks that arrives at conclusions similar to ours. They also note that, although professional standards exist for *testing* (AERA, APA, & NCME, 1985), none are available for other forms of assessment (Frisbie & Friedman, 1987; Della-Piana, 1985; both point out the irrelevance of the APA standards to classroom assessment).

Educational psychology. Most teachers take a foundation course in educational psychology, which includes one or more chapters on assessment. Psychometric concepts and techniques are generally highlighted; reliability and validity (in that order) occur early in the assessment sections, and receive a significant number of pages (reliability more than validity).

The books describe standardized tests, often in considerable detail, as the archetype of psychometric principles. Teacher-made tests (the label most frequently employed to introduce teacher assessment) are typically in "second place." Some writers portray teacher-made tests as clearly inferior to published instruments (e.g., Hudgins, et al., 1983), but teacher judgments more often appear as plausible alternatives.

Assessment of "what" is an important consideration, of course. Texts generally stress the importance of defining outcomes as behavioral objectives: "The step that usually gives the most difficulty to evaluators is . . . stating objectives in behavioral terms. Such terms as know, understand, and appreciate are vague and open to too many interpretations" (Lindgren & Suter, 1985, pp. 376-377).

Other authors, more cognitively oriented, distinguish between instructional goals and behavioral objectives (e.g., Gage & Berliner, 1988; Glover, Bruning, & Filbeck, 1983). These texts allow the words prohibited above, but not to design assessment. Good and Brophy (1980), for instance, talk about goals falling in the areas of intellectual skill, cognitive strategies, information (knowledge), motor skills, and attitudes. They nonetheless agree with Glover, et al. (1983) that generalities must be converted into behavioral objectives. The texts often comment on sources of evidence other than tests—observations, checklists, interviews, anecdotes. But these topics receive little attention and lack any principled treatment.

The texts provide few examples, and those are seldom helpful or convincing. For instance, after stressing the importance of behavioral specifications, Lindgren and Suter (1985) discuss how a teacher might use observational evidence for the objective, "The student becomes interested in the history and culture of Peru" (p. 379)—a toughie for a behaviorist, but the authors' choice. As evidence, they suggest students' (a) persistence in questions about Peru, (b) lingering after class to continue the discussion, (c) asking for books on the topic, or (d) collecting stamps from Peru. While these are clearly "behaviors," the meaning of "interest and the link to instruction" is unclear.

We should also mention textbooks in *educational measurement*. More specialized and hence less often encountered by classroom teachers, these books may include sections on *classroom assessment* (e.g., Mehrens & Lehman, 1973, give a few chapters to the topic), but not always (e.g., Popham, 1981; Kubiszyn & Borich, 1984; Ebel & Frisbie, 1986). A few specialize in this perspective (Green, 1975; Hopkins & Antes, 1985; Gronlund, 1975; Tuckman, 1988; also see ETS, 1984). The latter describe alternatives to tests (e.g., observation and portfolios), but still focus on psychometric rubrics—creating or selecting "items," establishing reliability and (secondarily) validity, and so on. A similar pattern prevails in a book on measurement designed specifically for the reading teacher (Farr & Carey, 1986).

Comments by a reviewer of Hopkins and Antes seem broadly applicable: " . . . one must look a little deeper at concerns regarding what this text does not contain that would be of value to prospective teachers and their instructors" (Dunbar, 1987). A survey of pre-service courses in educational measurement by Gullickson and Hopkins (1987) supports this judgment: " . . . instruction is overly preoccupied with the teaching of statistics . . . [and] many students . . . will continue to be inadequately prepared for classroom evaluation tasks" (p. 15).

Reading textbooks. For elementary teachers, reading textbooks take as the starting point the basal reader and procedures for placing students in the appropriate basal level. Lapp and Flood (1978) are typical; they (a) describe the basal, (b) link student progress to the concept of reading level, (c) discuss how to measure passage readability (basals are already graded by readability), (d) describe standardized scores for placement, and (e) list alternate methods for diagnosis (e.g., informal reading inventories and cloze procedures). Their approach is practical and atheoretical.

A second theme in reading textbooks is the emphasis on assessment for diagnosis. Johnston (1985, p. 157) notes the tendency to attribute reading problems to student ability rather than the learning situation, hence *problem readers* rather than *reading problems*. Aulls (1982) covers assessment practices extensively. He begins by laying out the chief purposes of teacher assessment: (a) group placement in the basal, and (b) the identification of students with severe reading problems. Standardized instruments provide the basis for preliminary sorting (p. 577). Students at the bottom of the distribution receive more intensive testing by the teacher or a reading specialist. The first step is to document "broad determinants of learning" (pp. 583-585): vision, hearing, motor behavior, attention, general health, social and emotional signs. The second step is detailed investigation of oral reading skill. Aulls devotes 35 pages to this task. "En route assessment," which includes observations, anecdotal records, and checklists, receives brief mention as a base for alteration in the instructional program.

None of these sources provides a conceptual framework. The pre-service program provides no basis for teacher-as-researcher. The routine throughout is *set objectives-test-reteach-retest*. Nowhere is the foundation laid for framing hypotheses. Also missing is any sense of *design*, of variation in conditions. In contrast, the caution is to "keep conditions constant during testing." The consequence is that interpretation (and decisions) are procedural and routine rather than reflective and speculative.

What do teachers learn about reading assessment?

Against this background, how might we expect elementary teachers to handle the task of assessment for instructional decision-making? We would predict that they emphasize standardized instruments for placement and designation of disabled readers, rather than curriculum goals. We should expect uncertainty about the technical aspects of assessment. Elementary teachers are more oriented toward humanistic and personal concepts to begin with, and less interested in the standard error of measurement.

These predictions match teacher perceptions in interviews of elementary teachers by Fraatz (1987), and are consistent with other investigations (Jackson, 1968; Stiggins, et al., 1986). Fraatz's work is recent and her excerpts compelling. The image is that of teaching as a technocracy, more akin to assembly line than profession, coupled with the conviction that the teacher is the chief "policy maker" for critical decisions about individual students:

When I asked . . . who had most influence over reading instruction, I usually got the following kind of response . . . "Me. No one else is really significant, because there's not that much outside influence . . . I cover everything that's in the workbooks, and we go through the stories, but my emphasis is what I think they're really going to need . . ." (p. 20)

Instructional outcomes. Teachers' technical language is scattershot, reflecting exposure to piecemeal materials, and the absence of any overarching conceptual framework:

"I make sure that all of them have had phonics sheets, all the consonants, all of the blends. . . . Theoretically, I'd love to take each of the children and teach them, alone, say, the letter Q." (p. 24)

"We're just getting to left-to-right. Turning a page, you have to start on the left. That's why the room is set up this way—I hate rows, but it's to get them used to left-to-right." (p. 37)

Not surprisingly, teachers feel overwhelmed by the complexity of their task. Each student poses unique problems, and the effects of instruction are surprising and unpredictable:

"Sometimes, nothing works! Or else you find that . . . all of a sudden they know what they haven't known in some strange way, and you're not really sure how they figure it out." (p. 27)

Student behavior. Given the lack of principles and the complexity of their tasks, why do elementary teachers believe that they play a significant role in instructional decision-making? Standardized tests provide the base for sorting students into ability groups and readability formulas dictate the basal materials for each group. End-of-unit tests determine the pace through materials, and remedial worksheets together with extensions in the teachers' manual handle students at the extremes. What is left to the teacher?

The teachers in Fraatz's study answered this question clearly—basal materials and standardized tests dictate curriculum and instruction, but teachers handle the behavioral, social, and emotional dimensions (see also studies reviewed by Stiggins, et al., 1986, pp. 7ff). The second part of this arrangement makes sense. Students are not robots, nor are they clients or patients: "Unlike surgeons or dermatologists, teachers need active cooperation and engagement from their students, not just passive acceptance of a treatment" (Cohen & Murnane, 1985, p. 21). Standardized instruments may be silent on these matters, but teachers pick up signals. Their language may lack precision, but they clearly play a significant role by augmenting "numbers" with intuitive judgment:

> Children differ in self-motivation, in their maturity, in their work habits, listening habits, and abilities. With some children, if you go over it once or twice, they'll get it; with others, you can go over it ten times and they still won't get it. (Fraatz, 1987, p. 24-25)

> These children are certainly not limited in their ability; they're limited by their own social and emotional capacity to settle down to a first-grade reading program. . . . When they're in the room, you'll see them moving around, talking, forgetting to be considerate of others—it's just a hodgepodge . . . (p. 41)

> How many times does the first [slow] group say "I forgot my pencil, my barrette is coming out, my shoe is untied"—all these things that are interruptions. (p. 42)

These data are impressionistic, their reliability and validity are unknown, and they are seldom recorded in any systematic form. Textbooks provide little guidance. The technology of the basal and externally mandated assessments joins the teacher's behavioral and social assessments for decisions about students' academic future—assignment to a reading group, pacing of the group, instructional approach, placement in a special category. The technical core of schooling, the curriculum, is virtually absent.

What is possible?

The realities. The image of reflective and informed professionals working as a research team to help all students achieve high levels of literacy may seem an impossible dream. While current reform efforts rely on this vision, the realities seem contrary. Fraatz's pictures of teaching do not fit this model, nor do data from Wildman and Niles (1987). Intensive observations of 20 mentor-mentee pairs (a situation one thinks should foster reflectiveness) led them to several generalizations: (a) "observation skills and opportunities to analyze teaching are crucial aspects of a reflective life for teachers" (p. 26); (b) "most of their statements [from observations of teaching] were judgmental in nature and not tied directly to objective evidence" (p. 26); (c) "much of the knowledge they acquire about their classroom is tacit . . ., not explicitly described or consciously thought about" (p. 27); and (d) "teachers [eventually] saw the value of reflecting about teaching but found it difficult to put aside the immediate problems . . ." (p. 29).

Assessment is the key to accountability. We understand skepticism that evidence based on teacher judgments can be on a par with standardized tests. The trend both nationally and at the state level is for more mandated assessments. To the best of our knowledge, no parallel programs exist to enhance teachers' skills in assessment. None of the assessment programs being proposed provide for the judgments of classroom teachers in state and national data bases. Classroom assessments are not viewed as a sound base for policy making (Calfee, 1988).

We think a sound argument exists for changing this state of affairs. First, teachers *do assess* students today. They collect data and make decisions that influence the youngster's educational program. The need is to direct these assessments to encompass the curricular core of schooling, and to enhance the technical quality of the process. Second, the reliability coefficients of standardized tests may appear impressive, but teachers have the potential for assessment that is broader, more valid, and more reliable than current test methodologies allow. Finally, classroom assessment is a sounder foundation for guiding instruction. The teacher with knowledge and skill as a "practical researcher" is more likely to guide students to competence in reading and writing.

The barriers. We recognize the barriers in the way of realizing this vision. The procedures for teacher training, the routines of the basal reader, the conventions of the school, the methods of teacher evaluation —these and other realities are significant barriers. Pre-service preparation promotes a "follow the book" attitude, appropriate for some tasks but not the education our students need for the future. Once in the classroom, the problems multiply. Teaching is a lonely task. The day is spent with little people. Lack of a professional language provides limited opportunity for "grown-up" discussion of curriculum, instruction, and assessment. An alternative vision sees the school as a center of inquiry, a professional community (Schaefer, 1967; Calfee, 1987a). The concept of the teacher-researcher makes far more sense under these circumstances.

The possibilities. The challenge posed above is substantial—intellectually, technically, and administratively. But it is time to grasp the challenge. We have made substantial achievements during the past two decades in research on teaching and learning. This work is grounded in classroom experiments, and so many technical issues in "translation" have been handled. Finally, policy makers and administrators recognize the need for a fundamental change in educational practice (SRI, 1987).

Assessment of learning is perhaps the greatest challenge for the teacher. In the hands of the professional, assessment simultaneously illuminates student accomplishments, points out strengths and weaknesses in the instructional program, and sharpens the curriculum goals. This ideal presumes an informed professional and a supportive work environment. But the ideal is achievable, and may be essential for our future well-being.

References

AERA, APA, & NCME (1985). *Standards for educational and psychological testing.* Washington: APA.

Anyon, J. (1981). Social class and school knowledge. *Curriculum Inquiry, 11*, 3-42.

Aulls, M. W. (1982). *Developing readers in today's elementary school.* Boston: Allyn and Bacon, Inc.

Boyer, E. (November 19, 1986). On broadening the definition of language. *Education Week*, p. 20.

Calfee, R. C. (1987a). The school as a context for assessment of literacy. *The Reading Teacher, 40*, 738-743.

Calfee, R. C. (1987b). "Those who can explain, teach . . . " *Educational Policy, 1*, 9-28.

Calfee, R. C. (1988). *Indicators of literacy: A monograph for the Center for Policy Research in Education.* Santa Monica, CA: The Rand Corporation.

Calfee, R. C., & Drum, P. A. (1979). How the researcher can help the reading teacher with classroom assessment. In L. B. Resnick & P. A. Weaver (Eds.). *Theory and practice of early reading.* Hillsdale, NJ: Lawrence Erlbaum Associates.

Calfee, R. C., & Drum, P. A. (1986). Research on teaching reading. In M. C. Wittrock (Ed.), *Handbook of research on teaching* (3rd Ed.). New York: Macmillan.

Calfee, R. C., & Shefelbine, J. (1981). A structural model of teaching. In A. Lewy & D. Nevo (Eds.), *Evaluation roles in education.* New York: Gordon and Breach.

Chall, J. S. (1983). *Stages of reading development.* New York: McGraw-Hill.

Chambliss, M. J. (1986). The impact of assessment on curriculum. Unpublished manuscript. Stanford, CA: Stanford University.

Cohen, D. K., & Murnane, R. J. (1985). The merits of merit pay. *The Public Interest, 80,* 3-30.

Cole, N. (This volume). A realist's appraisal of the prospects for unifying instruction and assessment.

Della-Piana, G. (1985). The 1985 *Test Standards*: Consequences for the teacher-as-test-user. Paper presented at the Bergamo Seventh Conference on Curriculum Theory and Classroom Practice.

Dunbar, S. B. (1987). Review of *Classroom measurement and evaluation. Journal of Educational Measurement, 24,* 375-77.

Ebel, R. L., & Frisbie, D. A. (1986). *Essentials of educational measurement* (4th Ed.). Englewood Cliffs, NJ: Prentice-Hall.

Educational Testing Service (1984). *4 Keys to classroom testing.* Princeton, NJ: Educational Testing Service.

Farr, R., & Carey, R. F. (1986). *Reading: What can be measured?* (2nd Ed.). Newark, DE: International Reading Association.

Feigenbaum, E. A., & McCorduck, P. (1984). *The fifth generation: Artificial intelligence and Japan's computer challenge to the world.* New York: New American Library.

Fraatz, J. M. B. (1987). *The politics of reading.* New York: Teachers College Press.

Frisbie, D. A., & Friedman, S. J. (1987). Test standards — Some implications for the measurement curriculum. *Educational Measurement, 6,* 17-23.

Gage, N. C., & Berliner, D. C. (1988). *Educational Psychology* (4th Ed.). New York: Houghton Mifflin.

Glover, J. A., Bruning, R. H., & Filbeck, R.W. (1983). *Educational psychology: Principles and applications.* Boston, MA: Little, Brown and Company.

Good, T. L., & Brophy, J. E. (1980). *Educational psychology: A realistic approach.* New York: Holt, Rinehart, and Winston.

Goody, J. (1977). *The domestication of the savage mind.* London: Cambridge University Press.

Green, J. A. (1975). *Teacher-made tests* (2nd Ed.). New York: Harper and Row.

Gronlund, N. E. (1976). *Measurement and evaluation in teaching* (3rd Ed.). New York: Macmillan.

Gullickson, A. R., & Hopkins, K. D. (1987). The context of educational measurement for preservice teachers: Professor perspectives. *Educational Measurement, 6,* 12-16.

Haertel, E., & Calfee, R. C. (1983). School achievement: Thinking about what to test. *Journal of Educational Measurement, 20,* 119-132.

Heath, S. B. (1983). *Ways with words.* New York: Cambridge University Press.

Hiebert, E. H., & Calfee, R. C. (In press). What research has to say to the classroom teacher: Assessment. In A. Farstrup and S. J. Samuels (Eds.), *What research has to say about reading instruction.* Newark, DE: International Reading Association.

Hopkins, C. D., & Antes, R. L. (1985). *Classroom measurement and evaluation* (2nd Ed.). Itasca, IL: Peacock Publishers.

Hudgins, B. B., Phye, G. D., Schau, C. G., Theisen, G. L., Ames, C., & Ames, R. (1983). *Educational Psychology.* Itasca, IL: Peacock Publishers.

Husen, T., & Postlethwaite, T. N. (1985). *International Encyclopedia of Education.* New York: Pergamon Press.

Jackson, P. W. (1968). *Life in classrooms.* New York: Holt, Rinehart, and Winston.

Jennings, J. F. (1986). Improving American schools: A national perspective. Paper presented to the National Association of Secondary School Principals, Orlando, FL.

Johnston, P. H. (1985). Assessment in reading. In P.D. Pearson (Ed.), *Handbook of reading research.* New York: Longman.

Kubiszyn, T., & Borich, G. (1984). Educational testing and measurement: Classroom application and practice. Glenview, IL: Scott, Foresman, and Co.

Lapp, D., & Flood, J. (1983). *Teaching reading to every child* (2nd Ed.). New York: Macmillan.

Lindgren, H. C., & Suter, W. N. (1985). *Educational psychology in the classroom, Seventh Edition.* Monterey, CA: Brooks/Cole.

Mehrens, W. A., & Lehmann, I. J. (1984). *Measurement and evaluation in education and psychology* (3rd Ed.). New York: Holt, Rinehart, and Winston.

Olson, D. R. (1977). From utterance to text: The basis of language in speech and writing. *Harvard Educational Review, 47,* 257-281.

Piaget, J. (1970). *Science of education and psychology of the child.* Translated by Derek Coltman. New York: Orion Press.

Popham, W. J. (1981). *Modern educational measurement.* Englewood Cliffs, NJ: Prentice-Hall.

Ravitch, D. (1984). Value of standardized tests in indicating how well students are learning. In C. W. Daves, (Ed.), *The uses and misuses of tests.* San Francisco: Jossey-Bass.

Schaefer, R. J. (1967). *The school as a center of inquiry.* New York: Harper & Row.

Scribner, S., & Cole, M. (1978). *The psychology of literacy.* Cambridge, MA: Harvard University Press.

Shulman, L. S. (1986). Those who understand: Knowledge growth in teaching. *Educational Researcher, 15,* 4-14.

SRI (1987). *Opportunities for strategic investment in K-12 science education.* Menlo Park, CA: SRI International.

Stiggins, R. J., Conklin, N. F., & Bridgeford, N. J. (1986). Classroom assessment: A key to effective education. *Educational Measurement, 5,* 5-17.

Strike, K. A. (1982). *Educational policy and the just society.* Urbana, IL: University of Illinois Press.

Tuckman, B. W. (1988). *Testing for teachers.* Chicago: Harcourt, Brace, Jovanovich.

Wildman, T. M., & Niles, J. A. (1987). Reflective teachers: Tensions between abstractions and realities. *Journal of Teacher Education, 38(4),* 25-31.

Wilson, S. M., Shulman, L. S., & Richert, A. E. (1987). '150 different ways' of knowing: Representations of knowledge in teaching. In J. Calderhead (Ed.), *Exploring teacher thinking.* New York: Holt, Rinehart, and Winston.

Wittrock, M. C. (Ed.). (1986). *Handbook of research on teaching, Third Edition.* New York, NY: Macmillan.

The Wedding of Instruction and Assessment in the Classroom

MARGARET C. WANG
Temple University Center for Research in Human Development and Education

Many educational researchers have forecast improvements in class-room instruction as a result of advances in modern psychological theories, the broadened knowledge base in the area of human cognition, and stepped-up progress in the theory and technology of test design (Freeman [Ed.], 1986; Glaser & Takanishi, 1986). Yet these developments are of limited utility to program designers and classroom teachers as they attempt to assess student performance in an integrative way to improve instructional effectiveness and monitor student learning. If advances are to be made in the construction and appropriate use of student learning assessments, we need to have a better understanding of complex areas of competence and what constitutes effective instructional procedures. We must also be able to link this understanding to a knowledge base that includes ways to bring test development and psychological theories of learning and instruction to bear on the inner workings of the classroom.

In this paper I argue for the need to link an integrated approach to assessment and classroom instruction to the actual day-to-day implementation of school programs. My discussion is organized in four sections: first, extant practice in assessment; second, the major premises of the argument for an integrated approach to assessment and instruction; third, some of the relevant groundwork for continuing research and development in this area; and fourth, several of the major challenges to the development and implementation of an integrated approach to assessment and instruction. The paper concludes with some recommendations for further work in particular areas.

Extant practice

Researchers and practitioners alike have long grappled with the challenge to identify assessment procedures that inform instructional decision making and meet the learning needs of students (e.g., Glaser, 1963;

Messick, 1984; Tyler, 1950, 1967). Among the frequently cited reasons for assessing student learning are to:

- obtain certification of achievement;
- make instructional decisions such as placement, grouping for instruction, and selection (or exclusion) of students for special programs;
- provide motivation through corrective feedback to students;
- report progress to parents and policymakers;
- improve instruction and the curriculum of the school;
- evaluate program and teacher effectiveness; and
- make long-range predictions from rates of learning and development and thus to improve planning (counseling) for individuals.

Even though an underlying assumption of all of these reasons for assessment is to ascertain the quality or effectiveness of instruction, actual assessment practice typically affects the quality of instruction only tangentially. The use of assessment is limited almost entirely to policy and accountability concerns. Assessment of student learning, for the most part, has little effect on what teachers actually do during instruction, or how students proceed with their learning.

Thus, rather than playing an expanded role in the planning and refinement of the instructional process, the diagnostic potential of the many types of ongoing assessments in our schools has, by and large, been poorly tapped. In many cases, it has actually been misused (Heller, Holtzman, & Messick, 1982; Wang, Reynolds, & Walberg, 1986). The practice of matching diagnoses based on data from educational and psychological assessments to specific instructional interventions has been exposed as essentially more fiction than fact (Galagan, 1985; Reschly, 1987; Ysseldyke et al., 1983).

Achievement tests, for example, are often construed as functional for instructional decision making; test results purportedly are meant to help systematically determine the level of a student's competence in a given subject-matter area and plan for the next step in instruction. Yet even the most valid and reliable of the currently used indicators of this do not necessarily provide information about how students achieved their competence, the kinds of difficulties that they faced, or their present level of achievement in domain-referenced ways—information that is critical to improving the quality (effectiveness) of instruction.

We can expect to see more tests given for policy and decision-making purposes as a result of the current push for educational excellence and accountability. This increase, coupled with the current system for the identification and certification of students for special and compensatory education services, will likely result in a more glaring lack of connection among assessment, diagnosis, and instruction. Research and practical experience suggest, for example, that the educational plans that are designed and implemented for students with special learning needs, including the Individualized Educational Plans (IEPs) mandated for special education students, are often unrelated to the diagnostic information that determined their placement in special education or in other compensatory or remedial education programs such as Chapter 1. In fact, information from student assessments is more often subsumed by the administration and management of these programs than integrated with the substance of instruction (Allington & Johnston, 1986; Brophy, 1986; Heller et al., 1982; Reschly, 1987).

Premises of an integrated approach to assessment and instruction

Although there is some encouraging evidence of a trend toward the linking of assessment information to improving instruction, a major drawback remains: New developments in test construction and assessment procedures and the advances in research on teaching and learning have generally proceeded on separate fronts, and with little interaction with classroom practice. Classroom implementation of an integrated approach to assessment and instruction requires closer links in the work of several groups of professionals:

- psychometricians and measurement specialists interested in the improvement of assessment techniques and their relevance in enhancing classroom instruction;

- psychologists who are expanding our understanding and knowledge about the cognitive processes involved in acquiring subject-matter knowledge and in maintaining and retrieving information for further learning; and

- classroom researchers interested in improving the effectiveness and efficiency of classroom instruction.

Drawing on these and other relevant bodies of knowledge, several premises underlie the argument for an integrative approach to assessment and classroom instruction:

Premise 1: Recent theoretical and substantive developments have had a major impact on how individual differences in learning are viewed, the types of information on student differences that are examined and described, and the use of this information for instructional decision making.

Differences in students' achievement levels, learning approaches, and rates of learning have long been accepted as a given. However, the research questions and paradigms for investigating individual differences in learning have changed significantly, particularly over the last two decades. More and more, learner differences are described in terms of the manner in which information is processed, the mental mechanics and rules that students bring to the instructional environment, the motivation and affective response tendencies involved in the acquisition and retention of knowledge, and the knowledge and competencies of individual students. Although few of these "individual-difference" variables have been incorporated into the design of extant models of classroom instruction, there is growing support for their relevance to improving instructional effectiveness.

Premise 2: Effective instruction is an evolving process in which individuals interact with a fluid and complex learning environment that includes factors such as teachers' knowledge of subject matter and their ability to provide transformation of that knowledge to connect with the developing knowledge of students, teachers' behaviors and attitudes, and the demands of the curriculum on students' knowledge and skills.

There has been growing recognition of the dynamic nature of the instructional-learning process, the conditions under which instruction and learning occur, and the role of instruction in mediating distinct types of learning for improved performance. This modern conceptualization of student learning and instructional effectiveness emphasizes the teacher's role as a clinical diagnostician who is expected to identify the ongoing learning needs of individual students and make adaptive instructional decisions. Expert teachers respond with appropriate instructional actions to environmental cues, particularly student performance cues, that arise during the instructional process; they continually test this cue information against their own stored knowledge about students, subject matter, and teaching principles.

Premise 3: Successful students are motivated and active. They play a central role in planning and using the learning resources available to them. They acquire new knowledge and skills in a deliberate and efficient manner and use them in new learning.

There is a substantial research base that suggests a close relationship between students' ability to learn independently and their success in school learning. This research base also highlights the role of structured feedback to trigger students' self-corrective mechanisms and the significance of identifying the information requirements that will enable students to monitor and assess their own learning performance. Students' ability to play an active role in their learning could be greatly enhanced if they are provided with information to determine the type and amount of instructional support they need to achieve mastery of given curriculum objectives.

Premise 4: There is a vast gap between the state of the art of research and instructional innovation and the current state of practice in our schools.

One major reason for this gap is the failure of research and program development efforts to adequately address the technical needs of day-to-day classroom operations, and to provide the know-how for applying our best knowledge to the actual improvement of classroom instruction and learning. If our goal is classroom implementation, then an integrated approach to assessment and instruction must address the functional skills that enable teachers to design classroom environments and procedures that support the implementation of such an approach to improve instruction. A substantial information base on the content and consequences of improved practices is reflected in the literature and is found in extant in-service and pre-service training programs for school personnel. However, knowledge is sorely lacking about how to successfully implement innovations in classroom settings and support their institutionalization.

Future developments in the effective integration of assessment and instruction must take into account the implementation and training needs of classroom teachers and relevant specialists (e.g., school psychologists, special education teachers), as well as the changes in the organization and operation of schools which encourage new forms of practice by teachers.

Premise 5: Despite the advances in measurement techniques for assessing student aptitude and achievement, current tests typically are not designed to guide the specifics of instruction.

Test results generally provide information on global attainment and relative standing rather than prescriptions for improving students' learning. They have often been validated solely on predictive power rather than in terms of decisions about improvement of instruction, which they support. If an integrated approach to assessment and instruction is to be operationalized in schools with a high degree of precision, efforts during the next decade must include the development of a research base on the content and methods of tests that are directly related to the diagnostic-prescriptive process component of classroom instruction. This research base must also address the integration of assessment, diagnosis and prescription, and instruction across a continuum of individual differences and special programs (i.e., regular education; special, compensatory, and remedial education; programs for gifted and talented students).

Direction from the state of the art of research and practice

The prospects for acting upon the premises stated above are enhanced by recent methodological developments and instructional experimentation that aim to integrate the processes of assessment, diagnosis, and instruction. Selected efforts are highlighted here to illustrate some of the important considerations, as well as the available knowledge and technology, for developing and implementing a multifaceted, integrated approach to assessment and instruction. Among the salient design features or emphases of the innovative developments in this area are:

- curriculum-based assessment,
- assessments that include a dual focus on both subject-matter knowledge and metacognitive skills,
- an individualized approach to assessment and instruction,

- mechanisms and technologies that provide ongoing feedback to students regarding their learning performance,
- strategies that provide mediated learning experiences,
- systematic information management and retrieval strategies, and
- specific procedures for linking assessment information to the diagnosis and planning of instruction.

Dynamic assessment

Dynamic assessment is an example of a recent development that has implications for classroom implementation of an integrated approach to assessment and instruction. Under dynamic assessment, the interaction of student performance and teacher feedback includes the actual altering of instruction.

In contrast to conventional, static assessments of the products of students' learning, dynamic assessment is designed to delineate what has been referred to as each student's "zone of sensitivity to instruction" (e.g., Bransford, Vye, Delclos, Burns, & Hasselbring, 1985; Brown & Ferrara, 1980; Vygotsky, 1978; Wood, Wood, & Middleton, 1978). The integration of assessment and instruction under the dynamic assessment approach is accomplished by:

(a) determining the problem-solving processes used by individual students;

(b) identifying each student's responsiveness to learning new strategies and concepts, including his or her initial responsiveness and the extent to which knowledge is transferred to new learning situations; and

(c) prescribing instruction and learning activities that are optimally effective.

Task analysis

As in dynamic assessment, task analysis is a technique designed to improve instruction through carefully analyzing the structure of learning tasks. The application of this technique can be seen, for example, in the work of Venezky and Osin (in preparation) in developing a methodology for increasing instructional effectiveness in elementary school subject-matter areas.

The Venezky and Osin system is based on a series of mapping techniques for analyzing curriculum content and objectives, as well as the content of assessments. It focuses on the demands that instructional tasks place on students, the relationships between tasks and specific skills and topics, the manner in which tasks are taught in the classroom, and the manner in which task performance is assessed. Information from task analyses is used to answer two central questions:

1. How do the content and objectives of the various elementary curricula relate to each other? and
2. How closely does assessment relate to the content and objectives of individual curricula?

Scaffolded instruction

In many programs that train students to use cognitive strategies, ongoing performance assessment and feedback are facilitated by an approach commonly referred to as scaffolded instruction. Under this approach, students practice targeted cognitive skills, teachers evaluate students' performance and use strategies such as explaining and modeling to demonstrate the skills, and students are provided with additional opportunities to practice and apply the skills. The Kamehameha Early Education Program (Tharp et al., 1984) is one example of the incorporation of scaffolded instruction as a central part of a school curriculum.

Curriculum-based assessment

The curriculum-based approach is often incorporated in programs aimed at integrating assessment and instruction in a variety of subject-matter areas (Deno, 1985). Deno's procedures, developed most fully for use in special education programs, involve measurements directly at the "level of the lesson" or at the curriculum of the school. They involve no presumed underlying or predispositional levels, such as psychological attributes or social background variables. They assume that the most important level by far to have data for teaching is at the curriculum level—reflecting exactly how well a child reads now, for example, or how much mathematics the child has so far mastered.

The curriculum-based approach is also reflected in the design of the intelligent tutoring systems being developed by Glaser, Lesgold, and their associates (e.g., Glaser, Lesgold, & Lajoie, 1986). These systems build upon the computer's capabilities for adapting assessment and instruction to interactions with individual tutees (students), and for embodying "explicit representations of theoretical assertions about learning" (Glaser, Lesgold, & Lajoie, 1986, p. 35).

The interrelated sections of the intelligent tutoring program correspond with curriculum lessons, student aptitudes, and student knowledge. The multiple roles of the intelligent tutor are described by Glaser, Lesgold, and Lajoie (1986):

> At times the tutor plays the role of diagnostician, trying to decide what the student does and does not know. At times, it plays the role of strategist, trying to decide how to respond to the student's weaknesses by tailoring instruction. At times it plays the role of colleague or foil, interacting with the student as coach or adviser, or even as game opponent. (p. 35)

Computer technology

Computers have become an essential technological tool in the ongoing classroom assessment of student learning performance and outcomes, as well as in enhancing instructional effectiveness and efficiency. They are being used increasingly for test administration and for systematic, curriculum-based information management.

The Montevideo Individualized Prescriptive Instructional Management (MIPIM) System (Peterson et al., 1985) is an example of an experimental computer-based system for programming and monitoring student progress and for making referrals for a variety of instructional alternatives. The MIPIM serves the function of information management in a district-wide approach to curriculum-based assessment. The resulting data base is used to set instructional goals for individual students and to make decisions regarding the amount and type of instructional intervention required by each student.

This system, while totally domain-referenced, yields an important kind of norm-referenced information simply by noting how much time students take to reach any given level of achievement. The time variable emerges secondarily from data on when students enter and complete various sequenced segments of instruction. Thus, the norm-referenced data can be generated from ongoing records of student progress and therefore do not require additional student time for assessment.

Challenges and recommendations

As suggested in the preceding discussions of knowledge bases, programmatic developments, and technological advances, there is currently a wealth of information in the areas of assessment and instruction. Moreover, there is growing consensus, as demonstrated in part by the mere fact of this ETS conference on "Assessment in the Service of Learning," that we have passed the "prenuptial" stage and are ready to take concrete steps toward the wedding of efforts in these two areas. It is my contention, however, that the concept of an integrated approach to assessment and instruction will not make the quantum leap to widespread educational reality until certain critical challenges are faced.

CHALLENGE: To tie assessment to multiple factors, including the curriculum of the school, the cognitive processes of individual students, and the environmental context.

Research and development are needed to design assessment procedures that can produce holistic profiles of learning, instruction, and curriculum for individual students, and that have no adverse impact on learning for any one racial, ethnic, or gender group. The concept of assessment-in-context has been advanced by Tyler (1967), Messick (1984, 1987), and others as a means of providing a broad perspective of student learning performance and, consequently, linking appropriate instruction to the findings from student assessments.

Such multifaceted assessments would take into account a wide range of variables, including:

- subject-matter competence;

- learning processes and cognitive strategies applied as students acquire and use their knowledge and skills;

- structure and objectives of curricula;

- opportunities students may or may not have had to learn the assessed knowledge and skills or how to use information they have to acquire or monitor their own learning; and

- contextual characteristics such as features of classroom instruction, teacher effectiveness, the functional requirements or operating system of the classroom and of each student's home, and the general sociocultural environment of the community.

As Ralph Tyler so wisely noted two decades ago in his analysis of the gap between what we know and what we actually use:

> The accelerating development of research . . . has created a collection of concepts, facts . . . and methods that represent many inconsistencies and contradictions because new problems, new conditions and new assumptions are introduced without reviewing the changes they create in the relevance and logic of the older structure. (p. 13, Tyler, 1967)

The design of assessment and instructional programs based on the assessment-in-context premise would have particular implications for improving the current classification system for certifying and entitling students for special and compensatory education services. A case in point is the classification of students as learning disabled for special education services. The use of scores from intelligence tests and achievement tests to determine whether a student "qualifies" for special education support is a classic case of assessment not in the service of learning (Wang et al., 1986).

To achieve the goal of using assessment to improve instructional effectiveness, and thereby student learning, we must shift the focus away from a mentality of using assessment for labeling students for certification and placement into predefined categories of educational services. We must shift the focus to the identification of specific steps that could be taken to improve the quality of instruction for students with special needs.

CHALLENGE: To expand and clearly define the objectives of subject-matter curricula that foster the development of both domain-specific knowledge and higher-order cognitive skills.

Research and innovative program development efforts to date have shown that it is possible to create curriculum-based assessments for just about any subject-matter area or instructional domain. However, the effective integration of assessment and instruction requires agreement on the broad range of knowledge and skills that are essential for student learning. Research focused on subject-matter learning suggests that we need to examine further the knowledge and skill levels required to perform different tasks and acquire different types of knowledge.

The effectiveness of learning and instruction can be enhanced through specific attention to the kinds of knowledge structures or schemata that learners need to benefit from particular new learning experiences. Assessment of student learning would thus be based on a fine-grained analysis of how knowledge is organized in an individual student's mind, as well as detailed analyses of the task-specific knowledge and skills of a given curriculum area. Such work would hold great promise for developing and refining procedures for instructional diagnosis and planning.

CHALLENGE: To expand the repertoire of computer technology for facilitating the integration of assessment and instruction.

As discussed in an earlier section of this paper, recent advances in intelligent tutoring and other computer-based assessment procedures hold significant promise for an expanded role of computer technology in integrating assessment and instruction. One of the major impediments to the precise diagnosis of learning needs and the interlinking of assessment and instruction is the amount of information that must be acquired and stored on each student's learning performance and on the available possibilities for appropriate instructional intervention. Computers have the obvious capacity and potential for enhancing the capability of the classroom teacher to retrieve and utilize information on student performance and outcomes.

Computers can be programmed, for example, to adapt to the performance levels of individual students. This facility has two important ramifications. First, it means that assessment questions can be objectively selected based on responses to previous questions; computers can be used to interactively determine the various levels of an individual student's understanding. Second, by adjusting questions to a student's previous responses, the student is not repeatedly asked questions that are too easy or too difficult. As a result, assessment becomes more efficient and less time-consuming for both teachers and students. In addition, a greater variety of student learning attributes can be tested, along with multiple contextual variables, within the fixed time for assessment.

Although computers are far from being a panacea for totally objective, precise matching of student learning characteristics and learning needs to instructional alternatives, their capacity for curriculum-embedded assessment has only begun to be tapped.

CHALLENGE: To provide classroom teachers with the information and training support required to effectively perform a dual diagnostic and instructional role.

Good teachers know their subject(s) and their students. Yet few teachers come into the classroom with the skills to use this information for accurate diagnosis of learning needs and appropriate instruction on an ongoing day-to-day basis. Insofar as teachers and specialists, such as school psychologists, are the pivotal, on-line force for linking assessment, diagnosis, and instruction, attention must be given to providing the resources for effective implementation.

Continuing efforts to design improved assessment systems for classroom instruction should be aimed at developing simple, valid procedures that enable teachers to access and use relevant information in making instructional decisions. These assessment systems should facilitate the diagnostic-instructional process by making the feedback on student learning immediate and by indicating the appropriate next step in each student's learning plan. The information provided to teachers should point to strengths and weaknesses in students' cognitive processes as well as in their subject-matter content knowledge. It should help teachers evaluate the effectiveness of their own teaching by giving feedback on what students learn as a result of specific teacher interventions. It should enable teachers to identify both whole-class and individual learning needs.

In addition to accommodating these tangible information needs, assessment systems must take into account the conceptualizations of learning, teaching, and the curriculum that are held by teachers. Finally, they should enable teachers to share assessment data with students and to involve students in making instructional decisions.

While much research and development is needed to devise innovative ways to support teachers in sustaining implementation of both formal and informal assessment systems which are integrated into the instructional process, teachers need not wait for validated answers from research in order to begin tying assessment to instruction. Much can be done now:

- Informal assessments can be introduced, maintained, and elaborated through consultation with assessment specialists (i.e., school psychologists and subject-matter specialists, such as the remedial reading teacher).

- Simple assessment procedures can be developed for and by teachers.

- Teachers can use informal assessment procedures in simple inquiries (and/or research) to determine for themselves how well they accomplished the goals of a unit or semester, with appropriate structural and resource time and expertise (e.g., a computerized classroom record-keeping and management system).

Such informal efforts can produce sustained partial implementation in schools, while researchers proceed with designing and evaluating more complex assessment systems.

In a sense, developing teachers as diagnosticians is tantamount to training them to be creative researchers who use systematic techniques to probe and discover problem sources and solutions. Such training can help teachers identify the learning needs of individual students and make adaptive instructional decisions, both preplanned and on-the-spot decisions. However, the multidimensional qualities of classrooms, the diversity of student populations, and the large amounts of various stimuli and information in classroom environments make diagnostic instructional decision making quite complex. Findings from research on how teachers make instructional plans and on-the-spot, interactive decisions can have significant implications for the design of teacher-training programs. Such programs will improve teachers' capabilities to make effective curriculum adaptations based on precise information, both on the cognitive and social demands for effective functioning by students in the classroom and on the wide range of student differences.

Effective teacher-training programs in instructional diagnosis and use of improved assessment technology will be critical for bridging the gap that currently exists between the state of the art and the state of practice in educational assessment and classroom instruction. Training programs need to address the question of obtaining and using information and support to introduce and maintain an integrated approach to assessment and instruction. The training programs need to be tailored to address day-to-day implementation problems. The conventional "one-shot," in-service activities typically are not linked to the implementation and training needs of the school staff.

Final word

It is important to point out that my list of challenges is by no means exhaustive. It is, however, intended to convey the need for multi-perspective, collaborative efforts among those of us who, for too long, have been traveling separate roads to the improvement of instruction and learning. These challenges also convey the need to be mindful of the premise that assessment and instruction should be tempered by an appreciation for the overall educational context and for effective transitions while improving practice.

References

Allington, R. L., & Johnston, P. (1986). The coordination among regular classroom reading programs and targeted support programs. In B. I. Williams, P. A. Richmond, & B. J. Mason (Eds.), *Designs for compensatory education: Conference proceedings and papers* (Vol. VI, pp. 3-40). Washington, DC: Research and Evaluation Associates, Inc.

Bransford, J. D., Vye, N. J., Delclos, V. R., Burns, M. S., & Hasselbring, T. S. (1985). Improving the quality of assessment and instruction: Roles for dynamic assessment. Technical report. Nashville, TN: George Peabody College of Vanderbilt University, Learning Technology Center Technical Report Series.

Brophy, J. B. (1986). Research linking teacher behavior to student achievement: Potential implications for instruction of Chapter 1 students. In B. I. Williams, P. A. Richmond, & B. J. Mason (Eds.), *Designs for compensatory education: Conference proceedings and papers* (Vol. IV, pp. 121-179). Washington, DC: Research and Evaluation Associates, Inc.

Brown, A. L., & Ferrara, R. A. (October 1980). Diagnosing zones of proximal development: An alternative to standardized testing. Paper presented at the Conference on Culture, Communication and Cognition: Vygotskian Perspectives, Centre for Psychological Studies: Chicago, IL.

Deno, S. L. (1985). Curriculum-based measurement: The emerging alternative. *Exceptional Children, 52(3),* 219-232.

Freeman, E. E. (Ed.). (1986). *The redesign of testing for the 21st century.* Proceedings of the 1985 ETS Invitational Conference. Princeton, NJ: Educational Testing Service.

Galagan, J. E. (1985). Psychoeducational testing: Turn out the lights, the party's over. *Exceptional Children, 52(3),* 288-299.

Glaser, R. (1963). Instructional technology and the measurement of learning outcomes: Some questions. *American Psychologist, 18*, 519-521.

Glaser, R., Lesgold, A., & Lajoie, S. (1986). Toward a cognitive theory for the measurement of achievement. In R. R. Ronning, J. Glover, J. C. Conoley, & J. C. Witt (Eds.), *The influence of cognitive psychology on testing and measurement*. Hillsdale, NJ: Lawrence Erlbaum Associates.

Glaser, R., & Takanishi, R. (Eds.). (1986). Psychological science and education [Special issue]. *American Psychologist, 41(10)*.

Heller, K., Holtzman, W., & Messick, S. (Eds.). (1982). *Placing children in special education: A strategy for equity*. Washington, DC: National Academy of Sciences Press.

Messick, S. (1984). The psychology of educational measurement. *Journal of Educational Measurement, 21*, 215-237.

Messick, S. (May, 1987). Assessment in the schools: Purposes and consequences. Paper presented at the Inaugural Conference of the Benton Center for Curriculum and Instruction, University of Chicago: Chicago, IL.

Peterson, J., Heistad, D., Peterson, D., & Reynolds, M. (1985). Montevideo Individualized Prescriptive Instructional Management System. *Exceptional Children, 52(3)*, 239-243.

Reschly, D. J. (1987). Learning characteristics of mildly handicapped students: Implications for classification, placement and programming. In M. C. Wang, M. C. Reynolds, & H. J. Walberg (Eds.), *Handbook of special education: Research and practice: Vol. 1. Learner characteristics and adaptive education*. Oxford, England: Pergamon.

Tharp, R. G., Jordan, C., Speidel, G. E., Au, K. H., Klein, T. W., Calkins, R. P., Sloat, K. C., & Gallimore, R. (1984). Product and process in applied developmental research: Education and the children of a minority. In M. E. Lamb, A. L. Brown, & B. Rogoff (Eds.), *Advances in developmental psychology* (Vol. 3, pp. 91-141). Hillsdale, NJ: Lawrence Erlbaum Associates.

Tyler, R. W. (1950). The functions of measurement in improving instruction. In E. F. Lindquist (Ed.), *Educational measurement*. Washington, DC: American Council on Education.

Tyler, R. W. (1967). Changing concepts of educational evaluation. In R. W. Tyler, R. M. Gagne, & M. Scriven (Eds.), *Perspectives of curriculum evaluation*. Chicago: Rand McNally.

Venezky, R. L., & Osin, L. (in preparation). Fundamentals of computer-assisted instruction.

Vygotsky, L. (1978). *Mind in society: The development of higher psychological processes.* Cambridge, MA: Harvard University Press.

Wood, D., Wood, H., & Middleton, D. (1978). An experimental evaluation of four face-to-face teaching strategies. *International Journal of Behavioral Development, 1,* 131-147.

Wang, M. C., Reynolds, M. C., & Walberg, H. J. (1986). Rethinking special education. *Educational Leadership, 44(1),* 26-31.

Ysseldyke, J., Thurlow, M., Graden, J., Wesson, C., Deno, S., & Algozzine, B. (1983). Generalizations from five years of research on assessment and decision making. *Exceptional Education Quarterly, 4(1),* 75-93.

The Integration of Instruction and Assessment in Technical Jobs

ALAN LESGOLD
University of Pittsburgh

For several years, I have been working with Sherrie Gott of the Air Force and Susanne Lajoie at the Learning Research and Development Center on an intelligent computer system for training electronics technicians. Our system is a computer-based, coached practice environment: It instructs by providing practice opportunities that are realistic with respect to the representation of the job environment but sheltered in the sense that hints are provided by an intelligent coach. Such environments provide a special opportunity to assess training achievement continuously through recording of on-line problem-solving performance. Even without such a specialized environment, however, the mixing of assessment with instruction is generally becoming more possible and more enticing. This is especially the case with computer-based training and testing for business, industry, and military jobs.

As the field of psychological testing has advanced and as the psychology of instruction has improved, we have developed progressively more refined abilities to assess performance. This is especially true in areas where detailed cognitive analyses have shown the specific knowledge components that are necessary to various capabilities. This increased refinement of knowledge assessment, combined with a general orientation toward management by objectives, creates what appears to be a very rational approach to training: Develop a set of knowledge goals for the training and then alternate testing with training. Test to determine which goals have been achieved, and then focus training on the goals not yet achieved. In essence, this approach imposes a feedback loop on the training process: Do some training, assess progress, adjust the training regimen, and so on.

What we're talking about, then, is the interaction, in a training system, of two roles: that of the tester, who is concerned with longer-term educational goal-setting and evaluation, and that of the trainer, who needs to adapt the course of individual lessons to the trainee's capabilities. In designing a training system, we must pay attention to the information needs of both these roles. From the perspective of the traditional tester, an intelligent computer-based training system presents an interesting opportunity. Such systems, at least in some of their variations, operate by continually modeling student performance and comparing it to what an expert would do. So, ideally, an intelligent tutor continually knows just what the trainee does and does not know how to do. From the tester's perspective, it seems reasonable to ask whether the knowledge amassed by an intelligent tutor during the course of training might not occasionally be distilled into some sort of progress report.

The trainer's point of view is in the other direction, hoping the tester will help him or her out. Given the inevitable imperfections of any measurement, even that of an intelligent tutor, a trainer might ask whether tests should occasionally be given to provide a second opinion, outside of the training mechanism (whether human or machine), on how well, and in what directions, training is progressing.

Within a training system, the assessment mechanisms have a different purpose—to provide information to steer instruction. At the microscopic level, frequent, brief, and approximate testing is preferable to infrequent, standardized, highly-reliable tests. This reflects a basic truth about any control process: Steering knowledge that can feed forward to guide the ongoing process is at least as important as assessments that feed back with greater reliability but with delays. Very small bits of information of only moderate reliability are just fine, so long as they are available quickly. So, for example, the decision on whether to give a student a hint as she or he tries to solve a problem requires a quick but highly specific microanalysis, not necessarily a perfect or a fair one.

As the level of decision making rises, issues of reliability become more important. So, for example, the decision to add remediation in arithmetic for a clerk taking a bank's training course might demand more reliable data that is based perhaps on observations accumulated over some period of time. Finally, decisions of external evaluation—whether the training is any good, whether the trainee is fit for service—require not only high reliability but also attention to issues of fairness.

When using current intelligent tutoring-systems techniques for training, we note a particular form that this problem takes. Intelligent tutors maintain a continuously updated model of the student. This model is the basis for decisions about the selection of learning tasks for the trainee, about whether to provide coaching or other instruction to correct misconceptions the trainee may hold, and about the nature and extent of hints to be provided. After being trained on an intelligent tutor, then, a trainee has left behind quite a bit of personal evaluative data.

The question that arises is whether this data can somehow be the basis for an assessment of the trainee. As stated below, we must address some issues before we can give a positive answer to this question. It is worthwhile for me to describe the modeling approach we have been taking in order to help sort out the problems that would arise in using the student model as a means of assessing what the student has accomplished.

Student models

In our avionics troubleshooting tutor, which we call Sherlock, we made a distinction between two types of student models, a performance model and a competence model. By competence model, I mean a data base of information about general capabilities the student has acquired; a performance model is a prediction, based on the information in that data base, of the specifics of a student's performance for a particular problem task. Sherlock's competence model is based on its goal structure. Sherlock keeps a record, for each instructional goal, of how well the student has mastered that goal so far. Sherlock generates a performance model for each troubleshooting problem just before it is presented to the student.

The structure of the performance model is determined by what we call the effective problem space for the problem. The effective problem space is a representation of the steps, skillful or unskillful, that are likely to be taken by people trying to solve the problem. Both the optimal steps of an expert's performance and the likely missteps of novices are included, so the odds are quite high that the problem-solving activity of any student can be interpreted more or less as a path through the effective problem space. A student's performance model for a problem, then, is simply a notation for each step in the effective problem space, giving an estimate of how likely the student is to be able to carry out the required activity of that step.

Since we have mapped each step in the performance model onto one or more curricular goals, we can use the student's competence model to estimate which annotations belong on the nodes of the performance model. If a node in the effective problem space requires capabilities that the student is known to have, according to the annotations of the competence model, then we would expect the student to do well at that node in the problem space. If skills the student is known to lack are required, we would expect the student to do poorly.

We have so far used very crude annotations. For the competence model, we use *unlearned, perhaps, probably,* and *strong*, following a modified version of Anderson's (1983) learning theory. For the performance model, we use the annotations *good, OK,* and *bad.*

Going in the other direction, we can see that deviations of student performance from the expectations of the performance model represent marginal data about the competence model. If a student did better than expected, then perhaps the student has acquired more proficiency in a relevant curricular goal than we had attributed to him or her. If the student did worse than expected, then perhaps one of the competence model annotations is overly optimistic. While the many-to-many mappings between competence model entries and performance model entries leave some ambiguities to deal with, it seems possible to tune the estimation process sufficiently to allow it to work.

The approach we have taken seems to work sufficiently for our purposes, which are entirely on the training side. On the assessment side, we have used paper-and-pencil measurements to assess Sherlock's effectiveness, because the control groups in our studies do not have experience in the computer environment. So, all of our assessment has been with paper and pencil. Still, we can foresee the time when so much instruction and training will be delivered by computer that it will be very tempting to use information gathered by the computer during the course of training to provide assessments of the emerging competence of trainees for all the usual purposes, including job assignment, long-term training assignments, evaluation of training effectiveness, rewards for progress through training, etc.

Important issues

I turn now to some of the issues that I think are raised by this prospect.

First, let's consider the positive effects. For any given subtest or item score, we can certainly figure out the usual kinds of statistics, including some generalization of the concepts of reliability and difficulty. Indeed, C. Victor Bunderson at ETS speaks of the calibration of various measures, including measures generated by intelligent instructional systems. So, we should be able to say, at least, that successful performance at a particular node in the effective problem space of a training problem represents, more or less, the level of general proficiency that corresponds to a particular score on a general test of job proficiency. Now, it is only one error-ridden estimator, but it can be thought of as a vote to give the trainee a particular overall score. If there are many indicators, each "voting" for a particular score, then we ought to be able to cumulate this evidence and come up with some sort of central tendency to the "votes."

Thus, it appears, in principle, that training samples, like work samples, can be a source of assessment data about job competence. However, there are some special concerns that arise when one is looking at developing skill rather than already-established skill. The central problem is fragility. Different learning theories have different statements to make about the fragility of new knowledge, but the concept is pretty universal across them. Borrowing from Anderson's ACT* (1983) theory, we can see several forms of fragility.

First, a skill may have been acquired only at the verbal or declarative level. That is, the trainee may know what to do, but may have to think consciously about each step in doing it. Given any special problems that simultaneously require conscious effort, the trainee may fail to produce the expected performance. Also, the trainee's verbal knowledge may be encoded in such a context-specific way that it is not retrievable the next day, or when needed in the next problem. Competence, at this first, declaratively represented stage, may be temporary. It may totally disappear.

A second problem, not quite the same in character, is the automation of skill. With practice, skills become automatic enough to apply even when conscious processing capacity is being demanded by other special circumstances. So, even a strong indicator that a competence was manifest in the "clean" environment of training is not a certain predictor that it will be available in more realistic situations.

A related problem has to do with generalization. The move from learning in a training school to being tested, often in a different place, with problems that were not written to match the training exactly, requires an inevitable minimum of transfer that will not be required when scores are inferred from performance in the training context.

Another problem is the supportive nature of the training environment. There are many different types of training into which assessment might be embedded, and not all will have the same problems. The particular form with which I am most familiar is the coached practice environment. This environment affords opportunities to tackle hard problem-solving situations with the assistance of a computer-based coach. So, we get a chance to see higher levels of performance than we would usually find on a test, but we also must realize that success in our sheltered environments is not equivalent to success showing the same skill on an unassisted paper-and-pencil test. In a sense, we are measuring the opposite end from the usual of Vygotskii's "zone of proximal development" (i.e., the gap between what students can do on their own and what they can do with supportive coaching).

Finally, there is evidence that, under certain conditions, performance on computer-presented problems may be worse than with paper and pencil, exactly the opposite of what would be expected if training-embedded assessments from systems like Sherlock really are tapping the zone of proximal development, as suggested above. Hativa (1986) observed children using a testing and practice system on a computer and found that some low-achievement children benefited, in terms of paper-and-pencil achievement test performance, from time spent working on the computer, but they did not always show progress on the computer's own assessment scales. Hativa suggested that the need to enter answers via a keyboard, combined with response time limits and other similar constraints, resulted in systematically underestimating the capabilities of these children. For example, when adding up a column of numbers, we, in the U.S., write the digits of the answer from right to left, except when the answer is immediately apparent, in which case we write from left to right. The slower students in Hativa's study didn't catch on that the computer always expected the digits to be entered from right to left, so they were scored wrong on some of the easier problems. Also, these students were often the victims of time limits for responding.

So, for assessment purposes, we have a few problems using the performance of trainees as they learn from computer systems. The data are noisy, and they may be over-optimistic, because the supports provided in a training environment minimize near-transfer requirements, conscious processing-capacity limitations, and other forces that act to shrink the "zone of proximal development." On the other hand, each of these problems is really a problem of labeling. Something important is being measured; we just have to be sure we don't place it in the wrong equivalence class. A measure of assisted performance of a skill is not the same as a measure of unassisted performance. A measure of newly acquired capability is not the same as a delayed test. Measurements of the low end of the zone of proximal development are not the same as measurements of the high end. All, however, might be very useful.

Micromeasures of capability

So, it seems to me to be reasonable to do what Bunderson has suggested, to begin to calibrate the kinds of micromeasures of capability that are available automatically in computer-based training systems. By coupling on-line data collection with paper-and-pencil testing, we should be able to establish data bases that relate performance on the training computer system to predicted performance in more standard testing environments.

When we find that performance with paper and pencil is better than performance on the computer, we will want to study the quality of the training system's human-computer interface, because interface weaknesses seem responsible for known error in that direction. When on-line performance is better than our achievement measures would predict, the gap may represent a zone of proximal development. In such cases, students with lower aptitudes, who would be expected to have larger zones of proximal development, will require additional practice before they can manifest, off the computer, the potential shown by their scores on the computer.

The formula for realizing the dream of inferring achievement from performance during learning is complex. The trail left behind by a trainee who is using a computer-based practice environment consists of many fragments, each somewhat unstable and unreliable. These fragments, because of their numbers, can be cumulated if we can calibrate them to some already accepted achievement scale. However, we need to be aware that the blush of new learning fades a bit with time. Only knowledge that has manifested itself in multiple settings on multiple occasions can be assumed to be established with any permanence.

Further, the zone of proximal development spans performances between those on somewhat artificial achievement tests and those on overly supportive, computer-based practice environments. The high-aptitude trainee will look much better than a lower-aptitude peer on a paper-and-pencil test or in a novel performance setting, but, in a domain-specific sense, the trainee may not know much more. On the other hand, even after knowledge manifests itself in a low-aptitude trainee's on-line performance, considerable practice may be required before that knowledge is flexible and automatic enough to be useful.

To the extent that aptitude is partly the product of past opportunities for learning, using on-line learning data to assess progress in a training course may add a certain fairness to assessment. Once we know that a trainee has acquired the ability to exercise a skill with support from the computer, we have a legitimate basis for encouraging the trainee to keep practicing until the skill can be performed without support and in a partly novel setting. Measurements of the low end of the zone of proximal development, the standard sorts of test measurements we usually make, confound progress in training with the head start that the higher-aptitude trainee initially enjoys. So, perhaps we can learn to use the very data source that seems unreliable and potentially unfair to achieve a new form of fairness—the recognition of job-specific potential acquired in initial training.

References

Anderson, J. R. (1983). *The architecture of cognition*. Cambridge, MA: Harvard University Press.

Hativa, N. (1986). *Computer-based practice in arithmetic (TOAM): Dreams and realities—an ethnographic study*. Discussion Paper No.7-86. Tel Aviv: Tel Aviv University, The Pinchas Sapir Center for Development.

Lesgold, A. M., Lajoie, S., Eastman, R., Eggan, G., Gitomer, D., Glaser, R., Greenberg, L., Logan, D., Magone, M., Weiner, A., Wolf, R., & Yengo, L. (April, 1986). *Cognitive task analysis to enhance technical skills training and assessment*. Technical Report. Pittsburgh, PA: University of Pittsburgh, Learning Research and Development Center.

Assessing Technical Expertise in Today's Work Environments

SHERRIE P. GOTT, Ph.D
Air Force Human Resources Laboratory
Manpower and Personnel Division
Brooks Air Force Base

The study of skilled performance on complex tasks has matured as an area of psychological inquiry through a steady upgrading in task realism. Focus on knowledge-lean tasks, traditionally studied in laboratory settings, has given way to real-world, knowledge-rich tasks that require hundreds—even thousands—of hours of learning and experience to reach levels of expertise (Schneider, 1985; Lesgold, Feltovich, Glaser, & Wang, 1981; Lesgold, 1984).

Modern work environments—rich in human-machine interactions—are presently stimulating the growth of advanced forms of *technical* expertise, which has come to represent an important class of real-world, skilled performances. Research is presently under way in the Air Force to examine this form of expertise on complex, technical problem-solving tasks, the types of tasks that increasingly are defining our technologically complex society.

The Air Force work takes a perspective on skilled performance that distinguishes it from earlier expert-novice studies in the following respect: Attention is focused on the various intermediate stages of performance, as well as on the expert-novice extremes. More specifically, our fundamental goal is to accelerate the rate at which the practical learning experiences of apprenticeship result in progressively higher levels of cognitive functioning. Learning assessments and instructional methods to facilitate skill development are thus central to the effort.

Glaser (1985) introduced the concept of learning assessments at this very conference several years ago. I will argue today that the need for the types of diagnostic learning indicators proposed by Glaser does not end *after* formal classroom training is completed. To the contrary, the very specific and practical learning that occurs after formal instruction (in what

Lauren Resnick has called out-of-school learning) may bear a stronger relationship to success in real-world pursuits than does academic achievement (Wagner & Sternberg, 1985). My objective is to demonstrate that our tools for cognitive diagnosis and assessment are woefully incomplete until they include performance-oriented or practical learning assessments that can assist students and workers in developing real-world procedural and problem-solving skills. I will further argue that the importance of practical learning assessments continues to grow as out-of-school training programs flourish.

Evolution of practical internships

Historically, many occupations have included practical apprenticeships—or internships—as part of their training experience. Teachers, physicians, attorneys, psychotherapists, bankers, as well as craftspeople in technical fields such as carpentry, mechanics, and plumbing have traditionally been required to complete practice-centered internships. In theory, these programs should provide a fruitful source of assessment procedures that are practice- (or performance-) oriented. In reality, one finds only limited measurement work in this area that has advanced beyond a conventional approach of measuring factual knowledge. One explanation is that the rise of the vocational education movement in this country resulted in internships shifting back into the purview of school-based learning. The shift often meant that hands-on practice and coaching were replaced by direct instruction (Resnick, 1987). In turn, conventional procedures for educational measurement, which focused on declarative knowledge acquisition, were applied.

Meanwhile, a society of unprecedented technological sophistication was evolving, a society that now demands considerable specialized knowledge and competencies from its citizenry. These are the capabilities that in the past have been considered the purview of out-of-school training programs. A striking discontinuity thus exists between what the schools supply and what the real world demands as skilled performers.

Two major conclusions can be drawn from this brief historical account. First, the fluctuations in practical training programs highlight the "continuing tensions . . . between the 'formal education' part of training and the practical or clinical part" (Resnick, 1987). At the center of the sometimes acrimonious debate are issues involving the respective roles of the schools and the rest of society in training citizens for productive lives.

The second point is that while the gap has widened between what the schools produce as educated individuals and what the real world needs as competent workers, assessment has made only meager advances in measuring practical skills. To take the point a bit further, it is not unreasonable to suggest that the absence of progressive, skill-oriented assessment procedures may in fact be related to the demise of practice-centered training and the rise of more traditional forms of direct instruction. This is a viable claim, given the known influence of tests on instruction. Norman Frederiksen (1984) offered an insightful account of precedents in military training, where changing the test meant instructional reform. It may not be hyperbole, then, to claim that truly effective clinical training may never become a reality until valid assessment is in place to shape its curriculum.

Given the poor fit between models of school-based learning and society's need for skilled workers, it is not surprising that the industrial and military sectors have significantly increased their own training initiatives. American businesses are spending billions of dollars to establish and operate what have been termed "in-house corporate colleges" (Mitchell, 1987). It is estimated that as much as $40 billion a year is being spent to deliver instruction to eight million workers. For example, Motorola—a maker of electronic products—recently spent two years retraining its mechanical engineers for jobs as electronic engineers, because those skills are more highly demanded by information-age technologies (Mitchell, 1987).

Technology-driven instructional needs are similarly affecting military technical training. Interestingly, increases and modifications in technical instruction are most often found in on-the-job training environments, not in formal academic settings. In the military, the operational commands no longer count on the traditional models of school-based learning used by training commands to develop the technically skilled workers that are needed. Yet, even these programs—which clearly amount to a form of educational protest—bear startling similarities to the very (academic) models of learning they reject. Often the only notable difference is that the factual knowledge that fills the curriculum is more specialized in character. Still missing, by and large, are practice-oriented learning experiences and, as one might expect, accompanying practical learning assessments. As a way of speculating why this is so, let me contrast performance-oriented learning assessment with academic models.

Academic vs. practical assessment

School-based learning is directed toward the acquisition of theoretical knowledge and the development of general competency skills (Resnick, 1987). Glaser and others have argued that to be effective, academic learning assessments must target components of the developing proficiencies as informed by a cognitive theory of performance. Achievement components of interest might include:

- the structure and interrelatedness of declarative knowledge;

- the conditionalized nature of that knowledge, i.e., the degree to which it is associated with indicators of how and when it is to be appropriately used;

- mental models of task demands and task characteristics;

- theories held by students to explain certain phenomena; and

- automaticity of task subprocesses (Glaser, 1985).

In contrast, practice-oriented instructional programs are directed not at general academic proficiencies, such as knowledge of a particular subject (e.g., physics) or general computational skills, but rather toward some specific criterion performance, such as computer programmer or electronics technician. The level of achievement desired is beyond the initial stages of learning, where factual knowledge bases are constructed, networked, and preliminarily conditionalized, i.e., bound to conditions of applicability. Rather, emphasis is on the later stages of skill acquisition, where knowledge is proceduralized and procedures are in turn smoothed out via practice, that is, application (Anderson, 1982). Practical learning assessments should therefore be capable of pinpointing weaknesses in the proceduralization process, i.e., deficiencies in the learner's successive approximations of mature practice as demonstrated by increasingly conditionalized knowledge and efficient execution (Lave, in preparation).

Because the targeted level of achievement in out-of-school learning is a specific criterion performance, the nature of that performance has considerable influence on the design of assessment and instruction. The more overt and observable the elements of the criterion performance are, the more it lends itself to traditional forms of apprenticeship training and assessment. For example, a carpenter's apprentice can learn a great deal by following a traditional apprentice regimen of observing the master, executing a task with support and critique from the master, and then practicing extensively (Lave, in preparation). Similarly, assessment can be accomplished by evaluating observable behaviors and products of the behaviors, using standards provided by expert craftspeople.

An accepted principle of practice-oriented training is illustrated here, namely, that testing and training should mirror the criterion performance. The same principle applies for modern cognitive apprenticeships; however, as criterion performances become more mental and less physical, external behavioral elements are replaced by internalized cognitive processing, and the mirroring process is sabotaged. Learning through observation is significantly hampered; instruction and cognitive diagnosis are made exceedingly difficult. No longer is it effective to focus on overt behaviors and observable end products. Rather, practical learning assessments for modern work environments must be targeted at the internalized processes and concepts that lie behind the successive approximations of expertise. As with academic learning assessments, a guiding theory of performance clearly assists the clinical assessment process.

In the Air Force cognitive job skills project, we have been developing methodologies and amassing empirical data that reveal the processes and concepts behind various levels of modern technical performance. A theory of technical problem solving has evolved to guide our assessment and instructional activity. I will now turn to a more detailed description of that work.

Explication of real-world expertise

Imagine, if you will, some form of real-world expertise with which you are familiar. It could be a teacher or school administrator whose skill you admire, your attorney or physician, even your plumber or auto mechanic or the tennis champion at your neighborhood club. Chances are that the performances that come to mind are memorable because they are well-integrated and efficient behavioral sequences. Skilled performers are highly practiced; the rough edges or bumpy transitions from one segment of performance to the next have long ago disappeared.

Skilled performers are also goal-directed, so their performances appear purposeful and economical. There is, in other words, a quality of refinement and coherence about what they do. Real-world experts are also flexible and adaptive or, in other terms, well-tuned to specific demands. They appear to have a repertoire of particularized capabilities or subroutines to draw upon, depending on the specific circumstances and conditions. This adaptiveness means they are able to handle a broad array of problems effectively, even problems that may be new to them. Nothing seems to throw them off.

Keep in mind the characteristics of expertise I've just mentioned— coherence and integration of the performance, flexibility, strong condition-action bonds, i.e., actions that are precisely tuned to the particular conditions of the moment. These attributes suggest a holistic view of the studied expertise, where the performance as a complete entity is of interest.

One could also take a componential view where the component subskills of performance are the focus. For example, a physician's performance could be broken down into its various elements, such as knowledge of disease models and disease manifestations, knowledge of human anatomy and functioning, skill in surgical procedures, skill in human relations, etc.

We have found in our Air Force work that both holistic and componential analyses have been important to the explication of technical expertise. Practical learning assessments have subsequently been developed so that assessment targets not only the discrete components of skill but also the holistic performance. Strategic planning and efficiency (among other attributes) can thereby be evaluated.

Let me now briefly give an overview of the multiphase process we are following to get from a cognitive analysis of technical problem solving to a model of practical learning assessments. The sequence is as follows:

Phase 1: A hybrid knowledge engineering/cognitive task analysis methodology is applied to examine the problem solving of a range of performers (novices, intermediates, and experts) on authentic problem-solving tasks.

Phase 2: The results are synthesized to produce both componential and holistic descriptions of various approximations of expert performance. These descriptions in fact constitute a theory of performance and skill acquisition for the domain.

Phase 3: The derived theory guides the design and development of practical learning assessments, which closely resemble problem-solving simulations.

Phase 4: The theory also assists in developing scoring systems to address both componential and holistic aspects of the simulations. For example, both global strategies and localized tactics are scored.

Phase 1: Cognitive analysis of performance. We have used a hybrid knowledge, engineering-cognitive, task-analysis methodology to study the electronic troubleshooting of approximately 15 technical experts and 200 less-than-expert technicians in four electronics occupations. The cornerstone of the method is an expert problem-solving dyad. One expert poses a problem and simulates equipment responses to a second expert, who attempts to isolate the fault conceived by the first expert. The dyad format is extended by iteratively pairing intermediate and novice technicians with an expert who poses a problem and simulates equipment responses with each person.

The approach utilizes the effective problem space construct of Newell & Simon (1972) and a framework from knowledge engineering work in medical diagnosis to represent the mental events of troubleshooting (Clancey, 1985). With this framework, it is possible to analyze performance at both componential and holistic levels. In other words, both localized tactics and higher-level strategies can be examined.

During the real-time dyadic problem-solving sessions, the actions of the problem solver are recorded as discrete operations or procedures, e.g., tracing schematics or measuring voltage. (The actions are, in effect, instantiated components of performance.) Then, the reasons or precursors for the actions are expressed as the goals or intents of the problem solver. (They reveal the performer's higher-level plan or goal structure.) The interpretations of outcomes resulting from the actions are recorded as well, allowing the coherence of the sequence of actions to be examined. Finally, block diagram sketches of the equipment parts that are affected by the outcomes and actions are generated by the problem solver to illustrate the series of actions. These diagrams reveal how a technician's mental model of the equipment guides and connects the discrete actions that are taken.

Sequences of mental events such as these are called PARI structures (*P*recursor [to Action]—*A*ction—*R*esult—*I*nterpretation). An example of PARI data for a single action node is shown below:

Table 1: Pari Data

Precursor: Want to see if the stimulus signal is good up to test package cable.

Action: Measure signal at J14-28 with multimeter

Result: 28 volts

Interpretation: This is expected reading; this tells me that the stimulus is getting from the test station through the cable, so that part of the stimulus path is good.

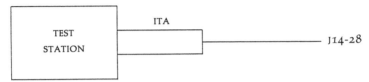

Notice in this PARI example that the Action element is a familiar troubleshooting procedure, namely, taking a voltage measurement with a multimeter. The representational formalism of the PARI framework does more than reveal that a technician needs to know how to take a voltage measurement, however. What is also captured are the conditions that surround such a measurement operation, including the reasons behind the action (". . . to see if the signal is good up to test package cable") and the interpretation of an expected voltage level (". . . tells me . . . that part of stimulus path [upstream] is good"). In effect, vital strategic processes of troubleshooting are made explicit with this representation scheme. The strategic plan that *produced* the measurement operation becomes known. In this case, the technician's plan is to constrain the problem space by eliminating either the stimulus or measurement (return) portion of the signal path.

We have found that by capturing problem-solving performances in real time, three important goals can be achieved. First, the proceduralized or conditionalized state of the technical knowledge can be established. This represents especially important input to skill training and assessment programs, given that conditionalized knowledge is a recognized hallmark of expertise. Novices, by comparison, may know how to use a multimeter to take a voltage reading (for example) but only as a discrete, isolated procedure. In fact, such procedures are often taught in isolation, separated from problem-solving conditions. What novices typically fail to do is produce the action under the appropriate circumstances, which suggests a weakness in the proceduralization process.

The second goal this form of knowledge engineering enables is the specification in explicit terms of the goal structure and strategic planning that further distinguish experts from novices. Plans and strategies are responsible for the coherent, refined performances we notice in experts. Goal directedness, in fact, appears to be strongly driven by the quality of underlying conceptual support knowledge.

Fully specifying that element of expertise is the third goal that is achieved with this approach. In the case of our electronics technicians, conceptual support knowledge takes the form of internalized, functional models of the equipment. These mental models provide the basis for both plans and actions by serving as the technicians' theories of equipment functioning and related fault-isolation procedures. They also enable the expert's adaptiveness to novel problems by providing an inferencing base.

A superstructure for organizing the system knowledge, procedures, and strategies of electronic troubleshooting which are yielded by this approach is described in Phase 2.

Phase 2: Derivation of a theory of technical expertise. A cognitive-skills architecture has evolved from our work to date to serve as an abstracted theory of the technical performance we are examining (Figure 1). The architecture highlights the important interplay among strategy, tactics (procedures), and conceptual (system) knowledge in this domain. These dynamic components and the resultant integrated problem-solving performance they produce are the targets of the practical learning assessments to be discussed next. First, let me elaborate a bit on the theoretical architecture.

It consists of three components: a Strategic Knowledge component, which sits on top of two interacting components—Procedures (Tactics) and System Knowledge. In this configuration, a top-level plan or strategy deploys pieces of knowledge and procedural subroutines as needed and as driven by strategic decision factors such as time and resource efficiency. Troubleshooting is thereby represented as multilevel, complex decision making, which involves choices among various top-level and intermediate-level strategies, as well as among alternative localized tactics. The choices are driven by one's level of understanding of the functioning equipment, as well as by knowledge of the likely sources of malfunction. Skill acquisition in this domain involves developing the component subskills by establishing and strengthening their strategic interplay. Practical learning assessments should thus target those components and processes.

Figure 1

Phases 3/4: Design/Development/Scoring of practical learning assessments.
The design of practical learning assessments in this effort has been
affected by several major influences: the theory of technical expertise
presented above, the principle in apprenticeship training/testing to mirror
the criterion performance, and prior work in medical education and
licensing, where clinical problem-solving skills have been assessed using
standardized simulations (Berven, 1985). The latter influence represents a
rare example in educational measurement, where advances have moved
assessment beyond a conventional, factual knowledge orientation.

In brief, we have used the derived theory of technical performance to
focus the assessment on Strategic Knowledge, Procedures, and System
Knowledge components, as well as on the interplay of these components
and the knowledge proceduralization process. It is with the latter that we
achieve a holistic evaluation. We have adapted and standardized the
verbal troubleshooting procedures used in our knowledge engineering
phase as a way of mirroring the criterion performance in testing. We have
also drawn upon the patient-management-problem methodology used in
medical education and credentialing in a special application to computer-
ize the learning assessment process (Hambleton, 1986).

To illustrate the nature of the diagnostic information provided to the
learner with this type of assessment, let me return to the PARI data example
in Table 1 above. Remember this example is only one of a series of 10 up
to 30 or 40 action nodes that would be explicated for a given troubleshooting problem. A sampling of componential diagnostic feedback
would be as follows:

(1) **Procedures:**
   —appropriateness/efficiency of voltage measurement
   —accuracy of schematic tracing to identify measurement point
   —accuracy of measurement outcome expectation, i.e., 28 volts
(2) **System Knowledge**
   —accuracy of mental model of equipment
   —accuracy of measurement outcome interpretation, i.e., that stimulus following the specified path
(3) **Strategic Knowledge**
   —reasonableness of goal (as stated in Precursor)
   —appropriateness of intermediate-level space-splitting strategy
   —efficiency of measurement procedure (versus swapping or some other procedure)

From a holistic perspective, it has been possible for us to evaluate the logic, systematicity, thoroughness, and efficiency of the complete sequence of problem-solving actions in terms of factors such as:

(1) Reasonableness/efficiency of approach in investigating the equipment (order followed in ruling out equipment components)

(2) Time and resource efficiency (labor, parts)

(3) Danger incurred (to self or equipment)

(4) Success in isolating the fault

My Air Force colleague in this project, Bob Pokorny, has developed an objective scoring scheme to handle this type of data. He has used a quasi-policy-capturing approach wherein senior experienced shop technicians:

(1) examine anonymous traces of PARI-like information for a given troubleshooting problem,

(2) rank order the traces in terms of goodness of the series of actions to isolate the particular fail,

(3) ascribe points to each trace, and

(4) provide a rationale to explain how points were credited or deducted.

Ratings of multiple experts on the same data set have produced interrater correlations in the 70s. The current version of the objective scoring scheme similarly correlates in the 70s with experts' ratings. We are continuing to attempt to improve both interrater agreement among experts and their agreement with an objective scoring system.

Conclusions

I have been pursuing two goals in my talk today. First, I have argued that diagnostic learning assessments are critically needed to enable the development of the problem-solving and procedural skills that are needed by a modern society. Given the known influence of tests on instruction, practice-centered training may never reach optimal levels of effectiveness without cognitive theory-based, practical learning assessments to inform and shape the instruction. The assessments should target the concepts and processes that underlie successive approximations of mature practice, and analysis should occur at both componential and holistic levels.

Assessment that operates exclusively at the component level repeats the all-too-frequent error in instruction, where a complex task is taught in piecemeal fashion but never as an integrated whole. We know that skilled performers use their strategic knowledge to sequence skill and knowledge components into a coherent problem-solving performance. Learning assessments must therefore target the performer's strategies and plans in order to foster advanced levels of skill.

My second goal has been to present the Air Force cognitive job skills project as a form of case study where practical learning assessments are being developed. They are a natural byproduct of the cognitive task analysis and knowledge engineering methods we have adopted and are thus grounded in cognitive theory. From earlier applications in medical education to the present use in technical domains, cognitive simulations represent a notable advance in educational measurement that deserves the attention of psychometricians and everyone else who cares about assessment that effectively fosters real-world expertise.

References

Anderson, J. R. (1982) Acquisition of cognitive skill. *Psychological Review, 89*, 369-406.

Berven, N. L. (1985). Reliability and validity of standardized case management simulations. *Journal of Counseling Psychology, 32(1)*, 397-409.

Clancey, W. (August 1985). Acquiring, representing, and evaluating a competence model of diagnostic strategy. Report No. STAN-85-1067. Stanford, CA: Stanford University, Department of Computer Science.

Glaser, R. (October 1985). The integration of instruction and testing. Paper presented at the 1985 ETS Invitational Conference: New York City.

Hambleton, R. K. (March 1986). Proposed steps for constructing and validating Air Force specialty diagnostic achievement tests. Research Plan for Air Force Basic Job Skills Research Project.

Lave, J. (in preparation). Tailored learning: Education and everyday practice among craftsmen in West Africa.

Lesgold, A. M. (1984). Acquiring expertise. In J. R. Anderson & S. M. Kosslyn (Eds.), *Tutorials in learning and memory: Essays in honor of Gordon Bower*. San Francisco: W. H. Freeman & Co.

Lesgold, A. M., Feltovich, P. J., Glaser, R., & Wang, Y. (1981). *The acquisition of perceptual diagnostic skill in radiology*. Technical Report No. PD5-1. Pittsburgh: University of Pittsburgh Learning Research and Development Center.

Mitchell, C. (September 28, 1987). Corporate classes: Firms broaden scope of their education programs. *The Wall Street Journal*, p. 27.

Newell, A., & Simon, H. A. (1972). *Human problem-solving*. Englewood Cliffs, NJ: Prentice-Hall.

Resnick, L. B. (April 1987). Learning in school and out. Presidential address at the Annual Conference of the American Educational Research Association: Washington, DC.

Schneider, W. (1985). Training high-performance skills: Fallacies and guidelines. *Human Factors, 27(3)*, 285-300.

Wagner, R. K., & Sternberg, R. J. (1985). Practical intelligence in real-world pursuits: The role of tacit knowledge. *Journal of Personality and Social Psychology, 49(2)*, 436-458.

A Realist's Appraisal of the Prospects for Unifying Instruction and Assessment

NANCY S. COLE
University of Illinois at Urbana-Champaign

Measurement specialists have been discussing for decades the need to make tests more useful for instruction. However, as this conference demonstrates, this elusive goal is still being sought.

Why is this goal so difficult to accomplish? In approaching this appraisal of the prospects of unification of instruction and assessment as a realist—from a practical perspective—I thought it would be useful first to try to explain the nature of the problem. With this more clearly in view, the paper turns to an analysis of the different and possibly conflicting perspectives that represent the problem—the measurement and instructional perspectives—to illustrate the characteristics of assessments desired from each perspective. Finally, the paper offers an appraisal of the prospects for unification of instruction and assessment, given these characteristics of the different perspectives.

What is the problem?

The topic of this conference is how assessment can serve learning more effectively. Presentations have included analysis of how assessment and instruction might be more closely meshed in the future and some practical, present-day illustrations of unification. The assumption most or all of the presenters make is that assessment can and should serve instruction. If everyone feels this way, why then is there a problem that this conference needs to address—why are assessment and instruction not already unified?

103

Current status

At one level, the answer is surely that they *are* unified. Teachers give tests in their classrooms, make informal assessments of students' progress, and use a variety of types of information, many of which might be called assessment information, to make instructional decisions, to monitor their own teaching effectiveness, and to give grades. In a national survey of teacher test-use that included interviews with teachers,

> [teachers] spoke of the many ways in which they assess students' progress and monitor the results of their teaching. Routine class and homework assignments, teachers point out, provide recurrent information on students' learning. Classroom interaction—during question-and-answer recitation and discussions, when students ask for help with their work, as they read orally or work problems at the board, etc.—yields immediate, continuous feedback on how students are doing. Special projects, presentations, and reports offer additional data on student progress and teaching effectiveness. Testing, then, is viewed by teachers as only one among the many strategies in their repertoire for measuring students' achievement.[1]

Furthermore, more than half of the 475 elementary teachers surveyed reported the use of students' standardized test scores as important in planning teaching at the beginning of the school year, initial grouping or placement of students, and changing a student from one group or curriculum to another. Slightly fewer of the 363 secondary teachers reported these uses, but substantial proportions (between 30 and 50 percent) at both levels reported use as well of district-continuum or minimum-competency tests. The greatest test use at both levels was of "Test included with the curriculum being used" and "Test 1 makeup," especially for deciding on students' report-card grades. However, the most frequently noted source of information at both elementary and secondary levels, with more than 95 percent of the teachers surveyed identifying it as crucial or important, was "My own observations and students' classroom work" (Dorr-Bremme & Herman, 1986, pp 36-37).

---

1. These authors note that to teachers, *testing* means "eliciting information from individual students, usually through paper-and-pencil instruments, under controlled conditions . . . periodically in time set aside explicitly for that purpose." By contrast, *assessment* of student achievement goes on constantly during the course of classroom teaching and learning" (Dorr-Bremme, Herman, 1986, p. 15).

Analyses of uses cited by the 44 teachers interviewed in this same study (p. 42) showed the top five most frequently cited tests used as follows:

- teacher-constructed tests,
- other major assignments,
- curriculum-embedded tests,
- standardized tests, and
- district objectives-based tests.

The most frequently cited uses for these tests were:

- planning instruction,
- assigning grades,
- within classroom grouping and individual placement, and
- monitoring students' progress.

In a questionnaire survey of 74 mathematics teachers and 62 science teachers, Harnisch (in preparation) found several supporting results. Teachers strongly agreed with the statement: "Classroom tests are important instructional tools. "However, they showed considerably less agreement (the ratings were near the neutral point on the scale) with: "Tests provide the primary basis for the student grades I assign." These teachers chose "test items to reflect my own instructional emphasis" and reported that "Student test results often redirect my instructional emphasis." However, they were neutral to the statement: "The availability of publisher-made tests should be an important consideration in the selection of curriculum materials."

In a survey of educators focused on testing in reading, Valencia and Pearson (in preparation) found some striking differences in response to questions about what *are* and what *should be* uses of testing data. Teachers acknowledged "decision-making about students" as a present use, followed closely by "evaluation/ranking of states," "of school districts," and "of schools." In the *should be* category, decision-making about students was joined with "decision-making about teaching" and "improving/shaping/determining curriculum."

These results, taken together, show a pattern of substantial use by many teachers of a variety of tests. However, the predominant reliance among tests is on those constructed by the teacher, and the predominant reliance beyond tests is on judgments and more informal assessments by the teacher.

Four additional results from the Dorr-Bremme and Herman (1986) study add further definition to the picture of the present status of test use. First, school principals report substantially higher use of standardized, norm-referenced tests and minimum competency tests than do teachers for four major uses: reporting to the districts, communicating to parents, curriculum planning, and informing the public (p. 31). Second, principals judge that the quality of present tests is generally high. Teachers agree, but less wholeheartedly, as they less frequently endorse the quality of commercial tests and more frequently express concern about the beneficial effects of the pressure testing exerts and the fairness of test results (pp. 66-67).

Third, both teachers and principals agree that "required testing has increased dramatically in the last five years" (at the elementary level about half the total testing time in reading and math is spent on state-mandated or district-mandated tests [p. 18]) and that "testing has led to more instructional time on the basic skills" (p. 64). Finally, teachers interviewed felt positive about tests when they related to classroom instruction and could be used to help individual students but negative about tests for other purposes external to the classroom (p. 69).

These results show a present context in which much testing is being mandated externally for purposes other than immediate instruction by the classroom teacher (e. g., reporting and accountability to various levels), in which such testing takes time away from instructional activities or more instructionally related testing, and in which the content of the external tests can and does exert influence on instructional content addressed by teachers.

The problem

At first glance, the results of this review of the present status of testing in the classroom may seem reasonable and appropriate rather than the source of problems. Teachers are relying more heavily on teacher-made tests and other forms of information for instructional purposes than on externally mandated tests. Surely this is appropriate. Teachers report fairly widespread use of externally mandated tests. Moderate use of tests not explicitly designed for classroom decisions could be viewed as surprisingly high.

Should it be even higher? Teachers and principals view the quality of tests (externally mandated and teacher-made) as generally high. Is there a quality problem hidden behind this general acceptance? Finally, there is a modest level of concern by teachers with the relevance of externally mandated tests for their use in instruction. Surely externally mandated tests are mandated for purposes other than immediate classroom use, so this modest level of concern is hardly surprising.

What, then, is the problem?

Three perspectives on the situation seem to be causing us difficulty as we pursue the unification of assessment and instruction:

Perspective 1: Standardized testing is primarily desired and mandated by agents external to the school and classroom, yet is more palatable to teachers and to the public if relevant to the classroom.

The first perspective derives from sources outside the school and the classroom, most frequently from district-wide or statewide levels. The level of information sought for external accountability purposes is generally more global than information sought by a classroom teacher for a decision on a particular day about an individual student. However, this testing is often done in the classroom and with time taken from classroom instruction time. Further, the results of the testing are often returned to the teacher at some subsequent time. Finally, having teachers accept mandated testing (at least passively) is beneficial to its implementation both politically and operationally.

Thus, making such testing as useful as possible to the teacher has the advantages of possibly helping the teacher and making the mandated testing process easier to implement. If the same test can serve the accountability function and also be useful instructionally, then one gets two desirable uses for the price of one and saves potential problems as well. Making externally mandated tests more relevant to the classroom is thus very desirable from the perspective of those doing the external mandating.

Perspective 2: Measurement specialists desire that testing and assessment have optimal measurement properties.

A second perspective comes from the measurement community itself, from those who study the theory and applications of measurement.

Note, however, that this concern for measurement properties is not to be found in the survey of current practice in the schools, based on reports of teachers and principals. Yet it is a common concern of measurement specialists that teachers should be taught measurement principles of objectivity, validity, reliability, test construction, and test scoring, as evidenced by textbooks and course syllabi designed for classroom teachers. Measurement specialists are concerned that assessments have good measurement properties and quite naturally believe that the measurement properties of classroom assessments as well as standardized tests could be improved by implementing this special knowledge domain.

Perspective 3: Teachers desire that testing and assessment be optimally designed for instructional purposes.

The third perspective noted here is that of the classroom teacher. This notion can be seen in teachers' concern that externally mandated tests are not optimally helpful to them, but as a proposition it goes well beyond that concern. The fundamental job of the classroom teacher is instruction. The tests and assessments presently well unified with classroom instruction are those that are seen as giving the teacher information relevant to instructional decisions, as motivating students to learn, as an almost incidental by-product of an instructional task, or as an assist in providing student grades. From this perspective, testing and assessment are viewed as part of the instructional process and judged as valuable or not to the extent that they further that process.

 Nitko (in press) noted that "Traditional approaches to disciplined inquiry in test design have tended to focus on optimizing the measurement efficiency of tests rather than optimizing their instructional efficacy." He argued that were the focus clearly on instructional efficacy, greater attention would be paid to a number of features not often explicitly attended to in test design. The "traditional approaches" cover well the joint perspectives of those who mandate large-scale standardized testing for accountability and policy purposes and those who are measurement specialists. However, the instructional perspective of the classroom teacher has not yet been well integrated with the other two.

If these three perspectives are correctly drawn, they lead us to what is surely the dominant problem in unifying assessment and instruction:

 Assessment is closely associated with two legitimate but different goals—the goal of measurement (and the accountabil-

ity and policy goals it serves well) and the goal of instruction. The fundamental problem then is the compatibility or incompatibility of these goals.

Characteristics of assessment designed for different goals

Here we attempt to analyze the characteristics of assessment implied by the goal of efficient measurement and those implied by the instructional goal to determine the compatibilities between the two goals.

a. Assessment designed for measurement

As already noted, the dominant goal from the perspective of the measurement specialist, as well as a goal also highly valued by the policy maker, is measurement efficiency. Thinking with respect to this goal of measurement efficiency is shaped primarily by the characteristics of large-scale, standardized, multiple-choice testing. This form of testing represents the most successful form of test design discovered to date to produce efficient, objective measurement. Large-scale standardized testing (whether school achievement testing, college admission testing, high school graduation testing, or certification testing) has prospered in the country as an efficient and objective means for measuring individuals or groups of individuals. In this context, its most valuable properties are its objectivity and its efficiency. Objectivity helps to ensure that individuals affected by the results cannot subvert them; efficiency ensures its affordability on a large scale. These two properties are beautifully meshed in the multiple-choice test.

In theory, validity and perhaps reliability should be the dominant characteristics of concern. In practice, they are important, but fail to dominate thought about measurement goals. Validity—does the test measure what we intend it to measure?—is difficult to assess, even when what we intend to measure can be clearly explained, and such purposes are rarely so clear. At best, validity is an ongoing evidence-gathering process that shapes our thinking about test-score meaning but rarely gives firm, clear, incontrovertible answers. Reliability is easier to study than validity, especially for multiple-choice tests, and thus often unfortunately gets greater attention than validity. Even so, politically, the notion of reliability is less dominant than the related notion of objectivity.

Because much measurement in education occurs on a large scale and is as much a political as a technical process, the characteristics we have come to associate with good measurement are a mix of theoretically defensible characteristics and practically resulting characteristics. Rather than to try to separate out the two sources of the characteristics, I have mixed them together below to represent the way the practical views of measurement typically mix them in our thinking. Most of these characteristics, if incompatible with instructional goals, will be just as difficult to alter whether theoretically or practically based.

The characteristics in Table 1 are closely associated with the function of assessment as efficient measurement. If the characteristics listed are not essential for efficient measurement, they are by-products of characteristics that seem to be essential for practical utility, if not measurement effectiveness.

Table 1
Characteristics of Assessment Designed for Measurement

—Valid. The most fundamental tenet of measurement is the requirement that measures be valid—that they measure what they purport to measure.

—Reliable. Effective measures must be reliable or reproducible on similar occasions, in similar settings, by similar test givers, on similar tests.

—Objective. The degree to which every observer will give exactly the same report on results (Cronbach, 1970) has assumed political dimensions that increase its importance.

—Cost-efficient. The dominant efficiency criterion for large-scale test use is likely that of cost-efficiency since testing is delivered to large numbers and often paid for by public agencies or a range of students with varying capabilities to pay. To be used, such large-scale testing must be inexpensive.

—Time-efficient. This characteristic refers to the time involved in giving and/or taking a test and, though related to cost-efficiency, can be distinguished from it.

—Centrally mandated. A testing mandate for a body of sufficient size is required to make the testing process economically feasible.

—Widely applicable. Economic feasibility requires that large numbers of users use the same test or same testing system so the test must be broadly applicable to a wide range of potential users.

—Centrally processed. Central development, processing, and scoring help to maintain assurances of objectivity and make testing economically viable for the central agency that collects fees for the testing service.

—Multiple-choice. This form of question is the best form yet developed for efficiency and objectivity.

—Machine-scorable. This characteristic provides the ultimate in objectivity as well as the scoring efficiency so critical to the affordability of testing.

—Delayed feedback. This characteristic is a consequence of other features (e.g., centrally processed) but is no special detriment to the measurement function per se.

—Used independently. Although test scores may be used in conjunction with other information, they are commonly designed to stand alone as an independent source of information rather than as a source integrated with other forms of information.

—Formal. A test is typically characterized by a formal set of procedures, given at a preset time to a large group of students, from published test booklets and administration materials, and results in pre-specified information or scores.

—Producing stable scores. The student achievement characteristics most commonly of concern in large-scale testing are viewed as reasonable, stable characteristics of students that would be expected to show minimal change over days or even a few months.

—Results designed for external user. The form and nature of the results are typically determined primarily by the needs and goals of the external mandating body.

b. Assessment designed for instruction

Nitko (in press) noted that there are less clear theoretical underpinnings to guide us in the search for theoretically desirable characteristics of tests designed for instructional use. In addition, the tradition of practice is not as publicly accessible as in the case of tests designed for measurement. Even to begin to identify characteristics of assessments designed for instruction, there must be some specification of what "designed for instruction" means. In this section, we probe in a preliminary way the implications of having the goal of instruction dominate the assessment, recognizing the tentative nature of the implications drawn and the characteristics named.

Consider what it should mean to say an assessment is designed for instruction. First, it would seem to indicate that the reason for having the assessment is an instructional one. The basic *raison d'etre* of the assessment is to further in some way an instructional goal. Second, promoting the instructional goal should be the primary criterion of the quality or success of the assessment. Although good measurement characteristics probably would be desirable in many instructional uses of assessment, the measurement characteristics would be subservient to the instructional characteristics. Third, all aspects of the development and implementation of the assessment would be guided by its instructional use. As Nitko (in press) noted,

> [this] includes considering how all of the following contribute to bringing about desired changes in students: (a) the type of test materials and their organization, (b) the tasks set by the test vs. the tasks set by the learning materials/procedures, (c) the timing and frequency of testing, (d) the usability of test results by the teacher, and (e) the way in which tests and test results will be perceived by students.

It should be made clear that many authors have been concerned about this issue of designing tests that would be relevant to instruction. This discussion is clearly not a new direction. Glaser (Glaser, 1963; Glaser & Nitko, 1971; Glaser, 1976) has written for two decades on issues of integrating instruction and measurement, and the popularized version of criterion-referenced tests that take their name from Glaser's work is the most widely used effort to link testing and instruction. Carver (1974) described the characteristic of being sensitive to instruction an "edumetric" test (as opposed to a "psychometric" test) should have.

Concern with content validity that reflects actual curriculum relatedness is another aspect of this same issue, as is the long-standing concern of many that test questions involve educationally important material (e.g., Ebel, 1972). Nitko's (in press) recent treatment, "Designing Tests That Are Integrated with Instruction," provides a broad view of the implications of concern with the instructional influence of assessment. The concept here, if different at all from these predecessors, is different primarily in the effort to consider the implications of a clear dominance of the instructional over the measurement goal.

What then would likely be the implications of the three guiding characteristics noted above for assessment designed for instruction? One complication in answering that question is that the nature of the implications depends on the particular instructional purpose. With the measurement goal we treated the measurement purpose that dominates practice—to measure global student achievement—as essentially the only measurement purpose in order to illustrate the dominant characteristics of measurement today. However, it is not clear that there is such a single dominant instructional purpose. Teachers report use of tests and assessments prior to instruction to gauge students' readiness; during instruction to monitor progress, make corrections, and provide motivation; after instruction to judge mastery and to give grades. Each of these instructional purposes would have different implications for the characteristics deemed desirable. Even so, in Table 2 a number of characteristics that appear likely to arise as desirable in one or more instructional uses are named to provide at least a tentative basis for comparison of the implications of the assessment goal in contrast to the measurement goal.

Table 2
Characteristics of Assessment Designed for Instruction

—Quality judged by effect on instruction. The quality of the assessment would be judged by the extent to which it actually assists in instructional tasks or ultimately in terms of the extent to which student learning is increased by use of the assessment.

—Design determined by instructional goals. The instructional purpose would affect all aspects of the design from the nature and form of the assessment task, to when and how it is administered, how it is "scored" and by whom, how results are reported and to whom, etc.

—Instructional *raison d'être*. The assessment would exist because it meets an instructional purpose or need.

—Teacher-mandated. The nature of the tasks, the way presented and used, and the nature of the results would be mandated by and meaningful to teachers.

—Adapted to local context. The assessment would fit the locally used instructional materials, the teacher style, and the characteristics of the students.

—Test tasks of instructional value. The student tasks from which the assessment information is derived would likely often be instructional tasks—tasks that have instructional value in themselves.

—Locally scored. Likely most classroom assessment designed for instruction would be scored locally, sometimes perhaps even by students themselves.

—Immediate feedback. Presumably the typical assessment would be designed to give rapid feedback to the teacher or student.

—Used with other information. Several types and sources of information are typically used together in instructional decisions.

—Informal. Much of the assessment would likely occur opportunistically at irregular times, without formal assessment materials or formal scores.

—Results subject to short-term change. At the level of day-to-day classroom instruction, teachers will often be concerned with skills and knowledge that can and do change over a matter of days and weeks.

—Meaningful to students. The nature of the tasks, the way presented and used, and the nature of the results would be meaningful to students.

A realistic appraisal for future unification

Table 3 presents the characteristics of the two perspectives side by side so they can be directly compared. It is clear that there are substantial incompatibilities in the characteristics derived from the two goals as presented here. Every characteristic on each list either represents a different goal or is in direct conflict with some characteristic on the other list. This conflict reaches from the nature of the test task and how that nature is determined, to the form of implementation, to the form and nature of the results. It includes as well differences in who is likely to develop, implement, score, and use the results.

Such dramatic incompatibilities clearly overstate the case. If the incompatibility were total, we would not see the present level of use of standardized tests in instructional contexts. The most extreme version of the differences has been drawn here on purpose. The purpose is to demonstrate a rather considerable incompatibility between at least some forms of the measurement goal and the instruction goal. To assume that the task of unification of assessment and instruction is an easy one requiring only minor adaptations in existing tests is to overlook these serious incompatibilities. If that assumption is made, then this appraisal is that the prospects for further unification of assessment and instruction are essentially nil.

However, it seems that we have concentrated far more effort to date on

Table 3
Comparison of the Characteristics of Assessments Designed for Different Goals

Assessment Designed for Measurement	Assessment Designed for Instruction
—Valid —Reliable	—Quality judged by effect on instruction
—Objective —Cost-efficient —Time-efficient	—Design determined by instructional goals
—Centrally mandated	—Instructional *raison d'être* —Teacher-mandated
—Widely applicable —Centrally processed	—Adapted to local context
—Multiple-choice	—Test task of instructional value
—Machine-scorable —Delayed feedback	—Locally scorable —Immediate feedback
—Used independently	—Used with other information
—Formal	—Informal
—Producing stable scores	—Results subject to short-term change
—Results designed for external user	—Meaningful to students

assessment designed for measurement than on assessment designed for instruction. Hope for further unification will come from developments from this more neglected latter point of view. A number of questions come to mind: Do teachers need or want better assessment for instructional purposes? If so, what forms would it take? Can instructional test design proceed without clearer, theory-based instructional design? Can present test developers steeped in the measurement goal contribute to designing assessment for instructional purposes or will those designs have to come from instructional experts rather than testing experts?

Answers are not offered here for these interesting questions. However, there are some positive signs about possible integration in the fact that there are beginning efforts to ask the questions and people continue to seek the unification of assessment and instruction. Further, over time, that seeking has increasingly taken an instructional perspective as you can see in many of the presentations today. This trend is the one that portends most positively for the prospects for unification.

However, to move further in this direction we will need to recognize the potential for incompatibility of our various purposes. We may need to consider more explicit identification of the fundamental goal for each situation first rather than trying to serve both instructional and measurement goals at the same time.

The prospects for further unification of large-scale assessment (based in policy concerns and dominated by the measurement goal) and classroom instruction are not rosy, this realist believes. However, there is more hope for unification of assessment built around concerns with classroom instruction. Even in this latter case there are many pitfalls in accepting the traditional characteristics of assessment coming out of the policy and measurement orientation. However, with a clear view of these pitfalls and work from the perspective of instruction, there appears to be at least the possibility of new forms of assessment that will be directly in the service of learning.

References

Carver, R. P. (1974). Two dimensions of tests: Psychometric and edumetric. *American Psychologist, 29,* 512-18.

Cronbach, L. J. (1970). *Essentials of psychological testing* (3rd ed.). New York: Harper and Row.

Dorr-Bremme, D. W., & Herman, J. L. (1986). *Assessing student achievement: A profile of classroom practices.* Monograph No. 11, CSE Monograph Series in Evaluation. Los Angeles: UCLA Center for the Study of Evaluation.

Ebel, R. L. (1972). *Essentials of educational measurement.* Englewood Cliffs, NJ: Prentice-Hall.

Glaser, R. (1963). Instructional technology and the measurement of learning outcomes: Some questions. *American Psychologist, 18,* 519-521.

Glaser, R. (1976). Components of a psychology of instruction: Toward a science of design. *Review of Educational Research, 46,* 1-24.

Glaser, R., & Nitko, A. J. (1971). Measurement in learning and instruction. In R. L. Thorndike (Ed.), *Educational measurement* (2nd ed., pp. 625-670). Washington, DC: American Council on Education.

Harnisch, D. L. (in preparation). Survey of educational testing in schools. Champaign, IL: University of Illinois at Urbana-Champaign.

Nitko, A. J. (1983). *Educational tests and measurement: An introduction.* New York: Harcourt, Brace, Jovanovich.

Nitko, A. J. (in press). Designing tests that are integrated with instructions. In R. L. Linn (Ed.), *Educational measurement* (3rd ed.). New York: Macmillan.

Valencia, S. W., & Pearson, P. D. (in preparation). Survey of educators' use of tests and test data. Technical Report. Champaign, IL: Center for the Study of Reading.